Library of
Davidson College

VOID

The Man I Pretend to Be

The Lockert Library of Poetry in Translation
Editorial Adviser, John Frederick Nims
For other titles in the Lockert Library see page 254

THE MAN
I PRETEND TO BE
☆ ☆ ☆
The Colloquies and Selected Poems of
Guido Gozzano

translated and edited by
Michael Palma

with an Introductory Essay by
Eugenio Montale

Princeton University Press   Princeton, New Jersey

Copyright © 1981 by Princeton University Press
Published by Princeton University Press, Princeton, New Jersey
In the United Kingdom: Princeton University Press, Guildford, Surrey

All Rights Reserved
Library of Congress Cataloging in Publication Data will be
found on the last printed page of this book

The Lockert Library of Poetry in Translation is supported by a
bequest from Charles Lacy Lockert (1888-1974)

"A Wintry Scene," "Totò Merúmeni,"
and "Ketty" appeared in the April 1980
issue of Poetry, copyright 1980 by
the Modern Poetry Association

This book has been composed in Linotron Bembo

Clothbound editions of Princeton University Press books
are printed on acid-free paper, and binding materials are
chosen for strength and durability

Printed in the United States of America by
Princeton University Press, Princeton, New Jersey

In memoria del mio padre
M. P.

Contents

Preface	ix
Acknowledgments	xv
Introductory Essay by Eugenio Montale	xvii

THE COLLOQUIES
  I. *Youthful Indiscretions*

The Colloquies	5
The Last Betrayal	9
The Two Roads	11
Ancillary Amours	21
The Game of Silence	23
The Good Companion	27
A Wintry Scene	29
Absence	33
Banquet	37

  II. *On the Threshold*

On the Threshold	43
The Fittest	49
Salvation	51
Paul and Virginia	53
Signorina Felicita	67
Grandmother Speranza's Friend	99
Cocotte	115

  III. *The Veteran*

Totò Merúmeni	125
A Woman Resurrected	131
Another Resurrected	141
The Honest Refusal	145
Turin	149
In the House of the Survivor	155
August Rain	161
The Colloquies	165

From THE ROAD TO SHELTER
    The Illiterate   171
    The Difference   185
    Parable   187
    The Intruder   189
    Strength   191
    Remorse   193
    The Last Renunciation   197

Uncollected Poems
    Parable of the Fruit   207
    Demi-vierge   211
    The Pattern   215
    Historia   217
    [Stecchetti]   221
    The Loveliest   223
    The Unenjoyed   227
    Ex voto   235
    Ketty   237

Notes to the Poems   245
Selected Bibliography   251

Preface

For readers of English, Guido Gozzano is the missing link of modern Italian poetry. His work—perhaps more than that of any other poet—represents the necessary step from the orotundity of Carducci and the strut and bombast of D'Annunzio, which held sway at the turn of the century, to the elliptical, understated, "hermetic" poetry that developed during and after World War I. In fact, Ungaretti's first small book of poems was published in 1916, the year in which Gozzano died. The critical enthusiasm for labels and for grouping poets into schools usually results in Gozzano's being lumped with the *crepuscolari*, or "twilight poets," of the first years of the century. In addition to the turn away from inflated rhetoric, he does share with them a certain languor and a certain love of the faded, a certain (actually, an uncertain) sense that nothing matters very much, that nothing is ultimately worth the effort necessary to attain it. For Gozzano (as for Sergio Corazzini and others of the *crepuscolari*), such attitudes were honestly come by: his tuberculosis, which was to kill him at age thirty-two, was the shaping fact of his entire adult life. But he transcends the melancholy mists of the crepuscular poets through his vigor and his wit, his intricate and often subtle harmonics, and above all his irony, which usually stings most bitterly when turned against himself. In his poetry, unlike that of some of his contemporaries, it is the sneer that starts unbidden as often as the tear.

Gozzano was born in Turin on 19 December 1883 into a fairly well-to-do family. His father's father had been a doctor and a prosperous landowner, his mother's father a senator and a friend of Cavour and Massimo d'Azeglio. Gozzano spent much of his childhood in the town of Agliè in the countryside of the Canavese, north of the city. The turning point of his adolescence came with the death of his father, an engineer, in 1900. Three years later, Gozzano enrolled at the University of Turin, ostensibly to study law, but he was soon caught up in the literature lectures of Arturo Graf and others and in the larger cultural life of the city. Before long he was publishing regularly in periodicals: poems, articles, short stories, fairy tales. In 1907 appeared *The Road to Shelter*, his first book of poems, and in that same year he met the poet and novelist Amalia Guglielminetti, who became "perhaps . . . the woman I could have loved"—though another poem written to her begins flatly, "It wasn't Love, no." In any event, it was Gozzano who broke off the romantic—though not the intellectual—connection the following year, and it is Gozzano whose poems tell us again and again that there were many loves, but no great Love. In 1911, he published *The Colloquies*, his best and best-known work, to an enthusiastic reception. Later episodes included a trip to India and Ceylon in 1912 (out of which grew the dispatches collected posthumously in *Towards the Cradle of the World*, his major work in prose) and the writing of silent film scripts (at least one of these—a scenario on butterflies—was produced, although an extended treatment of the life of St. Francis of Assisi was apparently never filmed). In the last two years of his life, he wrote more short stories and fairy tales and a handful of poems about the war as bad as most poems about the war. He also worked at a long, ultimately unfinished series of "entomological epistles" about butterflies, a poetic experiment that turned out to be more experimental than poetic. Then, after resigning from the world and resigning himself to the inevitable, he died in Turin on 9 August 1916.

The poems of *The Colloquies* are Gozzano's most characteristic work, in the character that he finally developed for himself. As he said in October of 1910 in response to a questionnaire from a periodical, its "poems—although independent—are joined by a fine cyclical thread. . . ." It is a book then, not merely a collection, a book in the way that *Dubliners*, still unpublished, was a book, and in the way that *Spoon River Anthology* and *Winesburg, Ohio* soon would be. Its setting is Turin and the subalpine countryside surrounding it, its characters a gallery of impressionistically sketched young women and a somewhat effete, sometimes tormented, occasionally astonished young man—

a young man who curiously prefigures, by several years, J. Alfred Prufrock.* He is a young man in flight from the corruption and aridity of his world and from something in himself that responds to that world, who at first resists and then finally comes to terms with his own ineffectuality, who sees his own life being lived by a "ghost of myself, young and well put together." It is characteristic of him that when he escapes into the pages of a sentimental novel from another time and place, it is one with an unhappy ending. It is even more characteristic of him, since he believes that beauty dies when it is possessed, to love most vividly that which is furthest from his touch: a young woman who kissed him when he was a child; a photograph of a girl fifty years his senior. When he seems to have within his grasp that which he professes to want—the "domestic wholesomeness" of a "vivacious little mate,/transparent as the air" and an anonymous existence in the countryside—he flees. The dream must never come true, lest the self disintegrate.

His most obvious rejection of the rather shabby world into which he was set down is expressed through his self-conscious role as Poet: the word "Muse" occurs with increasing frequency through the second half of *The Colloquies*. In "The Last Renunciation," the poem that concluded *The Road to Shelter*, Gozzano had presented a grotesquely funny exaggeration of the ivory-tower artist (who seems, incidentally, to do a lot more dreaming than writing) whose purity requires a total rejection of the bourgeois world and its emotional ties. The opening poem of *The Colloquies* presents the speaker as alienated from his own life, a "cold" sensibility who merely records the life he has never really lived. While poetry was originally pursued as an escape from tawdry reality, it has become a trap as well, since it inspires ambitions that are ultimately impossible to fulfill. In "The Illiterate" (Gozzano's "Resolution and Independence"), the speaker regrets that he ever learned to read other men's books and thus

---

* Another way in which Gozzano foreshadows Eliot is in his allusiveness. As his editors have documented, his poems are filled with echoes from Dante, Petrarch, Leopardi, and of course D'Annunzio. I have tried to re-create this effect in several places by working in echoes of lines familiar to an English-speaking audience.

became addicted to "such cunning flavors." In "Signorita Felicita," he seeks a more wholesome and simple life than he has found among the culture-ghouls of the city, but even in his moments of deepest feeling his head is filled with literary allusions; he senses his own artificiality, and once again his life is contracted to a few lines scribbled on a page. Finally, after various encounters with the "beautiful things that always told him lies," Love and Death, he comes, in the last section of *The Colloquies*, to a withdrawal that brings him a certain measure of peace, a peace that derives in part from a Wordsworth-like attachment to Nature ("Knowing that Nature never did betray/The heart that loved her"). The "dream of art" is abandoned, if only temporarily, and he recovers from his bitterness to accept as his new inspiration the figure of Punch, who symbolizes for him "the unimpassioned life,/small and serene, that doesn't venture far": he is not Prince Hamlet, nor was meant to be.

This ambivalence of spirit is shown just as strongly in the poet's attitudes toward, and relationships with, women. The earliest poem included here, "Parable of the Fruit," starts off with an epigraph from the Annunciation and proceeds to describe a fervor that is at least as much sensual as it is religious; from the same period comes the "unchaste virgin" of *"Demi-vierge."* But thereafter the two contrasting elements are kept strictly separate. The heroines of the longer narratives at the center of *The Colloquies*—Virginia, Felicita, and Carlotta—are chaste virgins chastely loved. Elsewhere Gozzano presents a gallery of seductions—successful, unsuccessful, and merely fantasized ("The Unenjoyed" is nearly one hundred lines of poetry devoted purely—all too purely—to the theme of sexual frustration). The culmination of this particular set of feelings and contradictions comes in "Ketty," a late poem more "Colloquial" than some of the pieces in *The Colloquies*: here is the envious admiration of health, vigor, and simplicity; the lust for a woman that he is incapable of loving; the quite sincere defense of art and idealism that is a bit self-consciously rhetorical; and above all, the uncanny ability to come away from any experience a frustrated fool.

Much of the time Gozzano seems to be his own most efficient enemy, but it is Time itself that emerges as the true foe. In the very first line of *The Colloquies*, he laments his twenty-fifth birthday as virtually the onset of old age, but the deeper irony was that at twenty-five Guido Gozzano had already lived three quarters of his life. His is a prematurely old poetry, a poetry of memories, of recollections: one of his favorite words is *rivedo*, "I see again." And yet in one important sense Gozzano won his battle with Time. "I want my image to be always young,/fixed at twenty, as by the artist's hand." He expresses this wish as he comes to the end of *The Colloquies*, and it has been fulfilled. It is a youthful image that stays with us, the image of a young man who is engaging and exasperating, energetic in language even when most enervated in soul, seeking through the form and polish of his verse to create that "momentary stay against confusion" missing from his emotions and his relationships. And Gozzano's achievement, small though in some ways it unquestionably is, is a real one. For his contemporaries and for his followers—among them the early Montale—he enlarged what could be said and enlarged the ways of saying it, and thus enlarged the possibilities of poetry itself.

Acknowledgments

Thanks are due to *Poetry*, which printed "A Wintry Scene," "Totò Merúmeni," and "Ketty" in its April 1980 issue, to Eugenio Montale, for his gracious permission to translate his essay on Gozzano, and to Giulio Einaudi Editore, the publisher of Guido Gozzano's *Poesie*, for permission to reproduce the Italian version of the text. During the time that this book was in the making, a number of people helped to make what is a lonely job somewhat less lonely, and I am happy to have the chance to record my warm appreciation to James Brophy, George Little, John Mahon, Leonard Poggiali, Stephen Sangirardi, and Barbara H. Solomon, most of them colleagues and all of them friends, who read some of these translations and discussed them with me; to Jon Cherubini of S. F. Vanni, who helped me find a number of important texts and provided detailed advice on publication; to Marjorie Sherwood of the Princeton University Press, who helped the book to find its proper shape and structure and offered constant encouragement; to Catherine Thatcher of the Princeton University Press, who worked hard and well to bring light to dark places; to John Frederick Nims, who provided many invaluable comments and suggestions on both the Italian originals and my versions of them; to Tom Pendleton, who with boundless energy and insight helped me work out both the largest and the smallest details of some of these translations; to Will Quinn, who was there from the start, sustaining, and reading everything with sympathy and care; and most of all to my wife Susan, who made room for Gozzano, who answered patiently and wisely hundreds of questions beginning "Which sounds better . . . ," and who shared—and thus redoubled—all the joys of the whole experience.

Introductory Essay by Eugenio Montale

The present volume contains all[1] of the poems of Guido Gozzano as edited by the late Carlo Calcaterra and by Alberto de Marchi in 1951, when Garzanti decided to collect the poet's works into one volume. That edition corrected not a few of the errors of earlier printings and above all restored to *The Colloquies* (according to Gozzano's intentions) two poems ("The Two Roads" and "Grandmother Speranza's Friend") originally published by Gozzano in his first book, *The Road to Shelter*. Thus was reconstructed the physiognomy of that book (*The Colloquies*) to which the poet owed his sudden fame in 1911; and it is on this text, probably *ne varietur*, although Calcaterra scrupled to say so, that tomorrow's readers, with other eyes than ours, will base their reading of the poet.

In the few pages that follow I will try to predict what their judgment will be. I speak of predicting; and everyone knows that predictions aren't always accurate. Why was Gozzano so readily greeted, on his arrival, with such exceptional recognition from the critics? Was there any validity in proclaiming him chronologically the last (but not the least) of our classics? If one reflects that, in a certain sense, every author is a classic who has mastered and perfected material that isn't his own, then one must frankly acknowledge that there was a validity to the judgment. One who aided in *The Colloquies*' success records that Gozzano "came into the public eye" in a way that is since no longer the case with poets—familiarly, with his hands in his pockets. Thus he seems to belong completely to a time before that much-lamented and hypothetical gulf that is supposed to divide the public

[1] The reference is not to this book but to Guido Gozzano, *Le poesie* (Milano: Garzanti, 1960); the original of this essay appeared as the introduction to that volume (which was not, by the way, a complete edition of Gozzano's poems). M. P.

from serious writers. Gozzano was immediately read and understood by the readers of D'Annunzio and Pascoli and the minor poets of the "Treves type," who were all more or less followers of D'Annunzio and Pascoli. And he was understood the way he wanted to be: his drama, his "croaking ghost wrapped in a fantasy," was taken very seriously, leaving to a few subtle initiates (Serra more than any other) the work of distinguishing between his real art and the theatrical cleverness of his "fiction."

And yet the fact that there was a distinction immediately tells us something. Gozzano fit into the public taste without arousing suspicion because he worked a sort of reduction upon the poetry that had come before him. He presented a new species of poetry, that poetry of *faux-exprès*, of semitones and harmonies in gray, that poetry truly not heroic but *en pantoufles* that the French, Belgian, and Flemish post-symbolists had already been experimenting with for so many years (Calcaterra has given a complete list of these poets); and much more than Orsini, Graf (the later Graf), Gianelli, and the others who were beating that path, he stayed close to the verbal impasto of the *Poema paradisiaco*, of the sounds and accents of D'Annunzio at his most crepuscular (*avant lettre*).

There's been much discussion about whether Gozzano was the first to import into Italy the poetics of "good things in terrible taste," the "bourgeois" paraphernalia of the new poetry; and it doesn't really seem that the early Govoni, Moretti, Giorgieri Contri and others were waiting to take the hint from him. But it's a pointless discussion. Gozzano underwent many influences: he was a D'Annunzian at twenty, and much later as well; he beseeched God in verse to deliver him from the lues of D'Annunzianism; he read those foreign poets who could best free him from that peril, but he was the only one of the poets of his time who knew how to give us his complete portrait in a brief collection of lyrics. In this way he was saved from his D'Annunzianism, or if you prefer, his incurable aestheticism. If he had tried to follow the premises of his new poetics to the end, if he had tried to give us, as others tried, a poetry of *grisailles*, Verlainish, spent, attenuated, he would no longer be remembered, not because of the incoherence of the enterprise but because of the instrumental difficulties he would have encountered (the same difficulties which, from Betteloni to Graf's undervalued *Rhymes of the Forest*, have encumbered every attempt, in Italy, at a poetry that would be humble and vernacular in a bourgeois way). Gozzano, however, had the shrewdness to be incoherent and to stop halfway. I don't even think that it was shrewdness; it was instinct. There was a verbal experiment in the air—plastic, lively, and new—that had found in D'Annunzio its supreme craftsman, and that, stripped down, led D'Annunzio into the liveliest parts of his *Alcione*. Gozzano didn't push himself as far forward as *Alcione*, he stopped at the *Poema paradisiaco*, and he wrapped the bric-a-brac of the good things in terrible taste in a sumptuously *négligé* cloak. He was, verbally, a rich pauper or a poor rich man. He reduced D'Annunzio as Debussy had reduced Wagner, but without ever arriving at results that we could call Debussy-like.

The poetry of Gozzano belongs to the climate that scholars of late eighteenth-century Italian theater call "verist," a climate that is for the most part of nondecadent origins. I realize that the step from this verism to decadent aestheticism is a short one and that both veins can be readily discovered in the same author (Albert Samain, the Puccini who leaps from *La Bohème* to *Turandot*, the Gozzano who goes from "Signorina Felicita" to "Paul and Virginia"), but it seems to me certain that in Gozzano's case the romantic-bourgeois-verist strain remained the most fruitful. Gozzano reduced the Italian poetry of his time to its lowest common denominator, and here once again the comparison with Puccini becomes irresistible. When we read *The Colloquies* with a fresh mind, we have to recognize that this poetry is neither the richest nor the newest of those years, but it is the most "secure." It's a small thing, perhaps, this poetry; but one can never doubt that it exists; whereas this doubt continually assails us when we reread D'Annunzio and Pascoli, who were so much more authentically lyrical than Gozzano.

Infallible in his choice of words (the first one to give off sparks by striking the aulic against the prosaic), the later Gozzano had the instinct and the good fortune to know he ought to remain what he was: a provincial aesthete, deeply Parnassian, a young and ill Piedmontese, D'Annunzian, bourgeois, but indeed Piedmontese and indeed bourgeois in his own way. I say that he had the good fortune because I doubt his intentions in this regard. The poem on *Butterflies*, to which he then turned his attention, shows clearly enough that after *The Colloquies* Guido Gozzano was exhausted. Even if he had discovered any new horizons, I doubt whether he could have found a fit instrument in himself to turn them into poetry. His most beautiful poems (and they are many) sing, but they don't sing lyrically like the best poems of D'Annunzio and Pascoli, and even more than they sing, they recount, they describe, they comment. And I believe that by now, at the distance of forty years, we can see clearly that when Gozzano wrote *The Colloquies* he instinctively grasped the unique position that was his; and that he was capable of this realization because, unlike those other poets who had influenced him (Graf included), he was born to be an exceptional storyteller or prose writer in verse.

And yet always a poet, we agree; and on this point a few words of explanation are necessary. Among Gozzano's critics, Gargiulo more than any other sensed the poet's prosaic base, but he forced his insight into deductions that seem to me unjustified, finally coming to maintain that Gozzano's major work was his prose (*Towards the Cradle of the World* and a few of the stories in *The Altar of the Past*). The truth appears otherwise to me. If one admits, as few admit, that in comparison with the Tasso of *Jerusalem*, the epic Ariosto is above all a supreme prose writer and storyteller in verse, then one ought to concede that Gozzano was, in his own time and within his own limits, the Ariosto of decadentistic themes that were not his own but that came together in him. It was his inclination to give form and artistic value to the material of others, and his classicism, his relative antimodernity is all here. I wouldn't, however, wish to create a misunderstanding: a verse that is "also" prose is the dream of all modern poets from Browning on, a dream that finds its possibilities in that integrity of style that makes Dante and Shakespeare the newest and most current of poets.

Now, Gozzano's poetry is not of this nature; it is a Parnassian poetry, and all Parnassian poets (I don't see any exceptions) are above all prose writers in verse. It's their way of making poetry, a perfectly acceptable way, and to understand this is to comprehend Gozzano, not to diminish him. Even D'Annunzio, Pascoli, and the early Rilke were not totally "modern" (that is, they were partly alien to the Browning-Baudelaire "junction" that is the source of all modern poetry), but their verse often sings at a depth at which Gozzano's verse never sang. Gozzano's verse is functional, narrative, a verse that fills and sustains the stanza and in which it is extremely difficult to detect any padding or to find those leaps and descents, that unevenness, that bathos, that are so common in grand lyrics. And yet there is a moment in rereading Gozzano when he seems to be all padding. From certain of his poems he cut entire stanzas without any damage, and there are other cuts that one could make; many of his stanzas could be repositioned without any damage, and others could emigrate from one poem to another without troubling us in the least. This seems to contradict what I said earlier, that Gozzano's verse is a functional verse; but in reality it doesn't. Altering his verses might produce a better or a different functionality, but it wouldn't destroy their basic character. Infusing a strong charge of auto-irony into the material of the *Poema paradisiaco*, Gozzano had the sense to keep his formal innovations to a minimum. He stopped where he did because another solution would have been premature, at least for him. He based his poetry on the collision, or "shock," of a psychologically poor, threadbare material, apparently fit only for minor tones, with a verbal substance that was rich, joyous, and very pleased with itself. This "shock" animates the brief psychological romance of Gozzano's that remains and in all likelihood will remain his true book.

Gozzano remained more of an artist than any other poet of his time; and he seems to have done so deliberately to exhume a distinction used, not always clearly, by De Sanctis, one that ought to be used with extreme caution in aesthetic discussions, since it can be the source of a great deal of misunderstanding.[2]

---

[2] The distinction that Montale would seem to have in mind is the one between the idea of a work of art and its manifestation; De Sanctis maintained that the true value of a work of art proceeds from the quality of its presentation, not the quality of its conception. Similarly, in judging the finished work of art, the critic must distinguish between its artistic value and any other value—moral, historical, philosophical—that it may possess. M. P.

An insertion of simple and direct "bourgeois" truth (his Piedmontese truth, in short) into that world of the *Paradisiaco*, where at certain moments we can still make out the stirring of Pre-Raphaelite figures, images of a late literary romanticism, and a slight lowering of the D'Annunzian tone: here is Gozzano, and here is his slight and firm originality, that, born as it was between 1906 and 1911, ought to have found itself very quickly short of material.

Reread the poem "The Road to Shelter"[3] (which gives its title to the book and which was reworked from an earlier lyric, "The Convalescent"), and you will realize that after that work—unsatisfying but nevertheless layered, rich, and promising—Gozzano embarked on increasingly limited investigations. His most secure poems ("The Two Roads," "Grandmother Speranza's Friend," "Turin," "A Wintry Scene," "A Woman Resurrected") have the perfection of a miniature, of an old engraving. It's a miracle that they don't descend into stereotypes. More complex and more digressive, "Signorina Felicita" reveals even in its metrics (which bring up to date the six-line stanza, that halved octave dear to comic poets) its essential character, that of a tale in verse; and it remains in the end Gozzano's most typical poem, though perhaps not his most balanced. Here, and even better in others of his poems, he develops through hints his catalogue of true women:

> She listened quietly,
> her hands held at the sides
> of her firm chin, her eyes
> fixed earnestly on me
>
> under her lashes' sweep, . . .
>
> ....
>
> I saw the delicate
> nostrils, I knew again

---

[3] Given the careful principle of selection of the non-*Colloquies* poems and the attempt to represent Gozzano at his best, I decided not to include this poem—especially in light of its length—in this translation. M. P.

> the expert lips, and then
> the little teeth that bit, . . .
>
> ("A Woman Resurrected")

> . . . brunette vivacious iridescent
> fearless in her cravat and upright collar, her brown
> hair flowing freely down from under her jockey cap.
>
> ("The Two Roads")

> "Stay!" And she held my arm against her side,
> the live links of her fingers eagerly
> twining with mine. "If you love me, stay with me!"
>
> ("A Wintry Scene")

This catalogue of true women extends from Totò Merúmeni's serving maid, drawn with Liotard's brush, to the modern horsewomen on bicycles whose ghosts we have just called up, firmer than the best figures of Boldini. And in comparison with these women, the more fully drawn figures of Felicita and Carlotta are immersed in a certain sickly-sweet mannerism.

In "Absence," you'll find a more lyrical Gozzano at last, but one who more closely resembles the other "harmonists in gray and in silence" of the beginning of the twentieth century:

> A kiss. And she's gone. She's away
> down there, where the path can't be seen
> in the deep woods, still making its way
> like a long corridor through the green.
>
> ....
>
> The pool is resplendent. And stilled
> are the frogs. But there flashes a spear
> of blue ember, bright emerald
> lightning: the kingfisher's here . . .

Here and elsewhere one senses how great a need Gozzano had to narrate an action, to weave a fable, even if that need alone was not enough to save him. The colonial rococo scenography, the style of eighteenth-century sylvan *folie* couldn't totally save the exercise of "Paul and Virginia." And one finds confirmation of Gozzano's inability to sustain a discarnate lyrical afflatus in nearly all of the blank verse of *Butterflies*, slack as blank verse always is when used by poets of a Parnassian temperament. One finds it also in the last part of "Cocotte," which contains some of his emptiest verses:

> Come! It will be as if you took my hand
> and brought me to the child that I was then.
> The boy will talk to the Lady once again.
> We'll rise together from time's distant land.

The Colloquies, then, don't lack stuffing; parts of the scheme that Gozzano outlined couldn't be filled in, suffused with the color of poetry. And only from a total renewal of his physical and moral life, after a lapse of years, could a new Gozzano have emerged, a Gozzano reconciled to God (so Calcaterra speculates, and not without justification). In what language could he have expressed his new sentiments? Certainly not that of *The Colloquies*. I say this, parenthetically, because converts, as a rule, are bad writers. It is nonetheless certain that Gozzano the consummate artist would have always distrusted those "good sentiments that make for wretched literature"—because he was literary all the way to the ends of his hair.

That he was such a one, rich with good culture, of restless but not illicit ambitions, is shown by those letters of his to Guglielminetti that for the reader of *The Colloquies* complete his image. These letters don't add anything to Gozzano's reputation, but on the other hand, they don't take anything away from it, as has been claimed. There Gozzano appears as he was: a gentlemanly boy, amateurish, sensual, not timid and certainly not at all introverted; a poet, in this sense, who was barely romantic and barely a "poet." A concrete, matter-of-fact temperament, with all the good qualities of a provincial bourgeois intellectual. Cultured, intrinsically cultured even if unexceptional in his reading, a first-rate judge of his own limits, naturally D'Annunzian, even more naturally disgusted by D'Annunzianism, he was the first poet of the twentieth century who succeeded (as was necessary then, and as it probably continued to be even after him) in "crossing D'Annunzio" in order to get to a territory of his own, just as, on a larger scale, Baudelaire had had to cross Hugo in order to lay the foundations of a new poetry. Gozzano's results were certainly more modest: an album of old engravings that will remain for the early twentieth century what Aloysius Bertrand's *Gaspard de la Nuit* remains for early nineteenth-century France, with so much less mystery, modesty, and magic, and so much more of our warm Italian blood. A limited and authentic book, totally incomprehensible to those modern intellectuals who are ashamed of Puccini and prefer *Falstaff* to *Il Trovatore* (but the only music that they love in their hearts is black music). And in this sense, yes—and not because he inlaid his verses with classical citations and loved his "trade" of poet—the last of our classics, or if you prefer, the next-to-last, the third-to-last . . .

Just as a good Persian carpet isn't left without a defect, I would like to leave some empty space in the Pantheon of poets, a few empty easy chairs, just in case two or three post-Gozzano lyricists might one day be thought worthy of occupying them. To see Guido again in his present whereabouts, to talk with him of Turin, to evoke once more those walks through the Valentino, those fine dinners at Molinari's and the Cambio (my memories of 1918, but Guido was already dead and I had never seen him), to hear the sound of his voice, with a Piedmontese accent, no doubt—what a temptation for a poet-man who even in the hereafter would want to find himself among men and not mannequins!

I'm not talking about myself, you understand. It may be that the chairs will never be filled.

THE COLLOQUIES (1911)
☆
I COLLOQUI

I
Youthful Indiscretions

☆

Il giovenile errore

I colloqui

> ... reduce dall'Amore e dalla Morte
> gli hanno mentito le due cose belle...

I

Venticinqu'anni!... Sono vecchio, sono
vecchio! Passò la giovinezza prima,
il dono mi lasciò dell'abbandono!

Un libro di passato, ov'io reprima
5 il mio singhiozzo e il pallido vestigio
riconosca di lei, tra rima e rima.

Venticinqu'anni! Medito il prodigio
biblico... guardo il sole che declina
già lentamente sul mio cielo grigio.

10 Venticinqu'anni... Ed ecco la trentina
inquietante, torbida d'istinti
moribondi... ecco poi la quarantina

spaventosa, l'età cupa dei vinti,
poi la vecchiezza, l'orrida vecchiezza
15 dai denti finti e dai capelli tinti.

O non assai goduta giovinezza,
oggi ti vedo quale fosti, vedo
il tuo sorriso, amante che s'apprezza

solo nell'ora triste del congedo!
20 Venticinqu'anni!... Come piú m'avanzo
all'altra meta, gioventú, m'avvedo

The Colloquies

> ... *a veteran of Love and Death, the two*
> *beautiful things that always told him lies* ...

I

Twenty-five years old! . . . I'm old, I'm old!
The prime of youthfulness has passed me by
and left its gift (and left me in the cold):

a book of the past, where I hold back a sigh
and find between the rhymes as I meander
the pallid traces of a brighter sky.

Twenty-five years old! The biblical wonder
is in my mind . . . in my gray sky already
I watch the sun start slowly going under.

Twenty-five years old . . . And soon the thirties,
unsettling murky flashes everywhere
of death along the way . . . And then the forties,

frightening days of the sullen, defeated stare,
then old age with his horrid limping gait,
with tinted hair and store-bought teeth to wear.

Youth never savored till it was too late,
now I see you as you were, I recognize
your smile: a mistress we appreciate

only in the sad hour of goodbyes.
Twenty-five years old! . . . The more I travel
toward the other end, the more I realize

che fosti bella come un bel romanzo!

II

Ma un bel romanzo che non fu vissuto
da me, ch'io vidi vivere da quello
25 che mi seguí, dal mio fratello muto.

Io piansi e risi per quel mio fratello
che pianse e rise, e fu come lo spetro
ideale di me, giovine e bello.

A ciascun passo mi rivolsi indietro,
30 curioso di lui, con occhi fissi
spiando il suo pensiero, or gaio or tetro.

Egli pensò le cose ch'io ridissi,
confortò la mia pena in sé romita,
e visse quella vita che non vissi.

35 Egli ama e vive la sua dolce vita;
non io che, solo nei miei sogni d'arte,
narrai la bella favola compita.

Non vissi. Muto sulle mute carte
ritrassi lui, meravigliando spesso.
40 Non vivo. Solo, gelido, in disparte,

sorrido e guardo vivere me stesso.

that you were lovely as a lovely novel.

II

But a lovely novel I could never be
the hero of: I looked on while another
lived it, my silent brother following me.

And how I cried and laughed to see that brother
who cried and laughed and acted the ideal
ghost of myself, young and well put together.

At every step I turned around to steal
a wondering look at him, eyes riveted,
spying on every joy and ache he'd feel.

The things he thought were all the things I said.
He comforted my sorrow in its shell
and did the living that I never did.

He loves his sweet life and he lives it well.
Not I, alone in dreams of art, who told
the lovely fable that I had to tell.

I didn't live. On silent sheets I unrolled
his portrait, marvelling silently to myself.
I don't live. All alone, apart, and cold,

I smile and watch the living of my life.

L'ultima infedeltà

Dolce tristezza, pur t'aveva seco,
non è molt'anni, il pallido bambino
sbocconcellante la merenda, chino
sul tedioso compito di greco...

5 Piú tardi seco t'ebbe in suo cammino
sentimentale, adolescente cieco
di desiderio, se giungeva l'eco
d'una voce, d'un passo femminino.

Oggi pur la tristezza si dilegua
10 per sempre da quest'anima corrosa
dove un riso amarissimo persiste,

un riso che mi torce senza tregua
la bocca... Ah! veramente non so cosa
piú triste che non piú essere triste!

The Last Betrayal

Sweet sadness, you were never far to seek,
not many years ago the milk-faced lad
nibbling a cracker, bent with a writing pad
over some boring exercise in Greek . . .

Later you were the only friend he had
on his sentimental pathway, green and weak,
hearing a girl walk, hearing a woman speak,
blind with desire, driven nearly mad.

Yet now from this corroded soul of mine
I feel the sadness fade away forever
before an endless bitter laugh, before

a laugh that makes my mouth a twisted line
of mockery . . . Ah, truly I can discover
nothing more sad than to be sad no more!

Le due strade

I

Tra bande verdigialle d'innumeri ginestre
la bella strada alpestre scendeva nella valle.
Ecco, nel lento oblio, rapidamente in vista,
apparve una ciclista a sommo del pendio.
5 Ci venne incontro: scese. «Signora: sono Grazia!»
Sorrise nella grazia dell'abito scozzese.
«Tu? Grazia? la bambina?» – «Mi riconosce ancora?»
«Ma certo!» E la Signora baciò la Signorina.

«La bimba Graziella! Diciott'anni? Di già?
10 La mamma come sta? E ti sei fatta bella!

La bimba Graziella: cosí cattiva e ingorda!...»
«Signora, si ricorda quelli anni?» – «E cosí bella

vai senza cavalieri in bicicletta?...» – «Vede...»
«Ci segui un tratto a piede?» – «Signora, volentieri...»
15 «Ah! Ti presento, aspetta, l'avvocato: un amico
caro di mio marito. Dagli la bicicletta...»

Sorrise e non rispose. Condussi nell'ascesa
la bicicletta accesa d'un gran mazzo di rose.

E la Signora scaltra e la bambina ardita
20 si mossero: la vita una allacciò dell'altra.

The Two Roads

I

Where row on countless row of yellow furze grew round
the Alpine road went down to the valley far below.

In a slow oblivion, coming rapidly in sight,
a cyclist appeared on the bright crest of the slope just then.

She approached us: she alit. "Signora, I'm Grazia!" She
moved toward us gracefully, smiling, in her plaid suit.

"You? Grazia? The baby?"—"You recognize me then?"
"Of course I do!" And then the lady kissed the young lady.

"My little Graziella! Already you're eighteen?
How has your mother been? And you've grown so beautiful!

My little Graziella: with such naughty, greedy ways! . . ."
"Do you still recall those days, Signora?"—"So beautiful,

and you ride here unescorted?"—"Just as you see . . ."—"My
 child,
will you follow us a while on foot?"—"I'd be delighted . . ."

"Oh! Allow me, if you will, to present the lawyer, a dear
friend of my husband's. Here, give him the bicycle . . ."

She smiled and she was silent. I pushed along the rise
the bicycle that was aflame with a rose garland.

And before me the fresh-faced child and the other one,
the shrewd wife, wandered on, arms round each other's waist.

II

Adolescente l'una nelle gonnelle corte,
eppur già donna: forte bella vivace bruna

e balda nel solino dritto, nella cravatta,
la gran chioma disfatta nel tocco da fantino.

25 Ed io godevo, senza parlare, con l'aroma
degli abeti l'aroma di quell'adolescenza.

– O via della salute, o vergine apparita,
o via tutta fiorita di gioie non mietute,

forse la buona via saresti al mio passaggio,
30 un dolce beveraggio alla malinconia!

O bimba nelle palme tu chiudi la mia sorte;
discendere alla Morte come per rive calme,

discendere al Niente pel mio sentiere umano,
ma avere te per mano, o dolcesorridente!

35 Cosí dicevo senza parola. E l'altra intanto
vedevo: triste accanto a quell'adolescenza!

Da troppo tempo bella, non piú bella tra poco
colei che vide al gioco la bimba Graziella.

Belli i belli occhi strani della bellezza ancora
40 d'un fiore che disfiora, e non avrà domani.

II

The one an adolescent in her short skirt, and yet
already a woman: brunette vivacious iridescent

fearless in her cravat and upright collar, her brown
hair flowing freely down from under her jockey cap.

And I, without a word, inhaled with the aroma
of the fir trees the aroma of that adolescent verve.

—O road to health (I said), O virgin apparition,
O flowering fruition of joys unharvested,

I wonder could you really make my passage here secure,
sweet beverage to cure the plague of melancholy!

O child within your hands you hold my destiny:
going down toward Death the way one goes toward peaceful
    lands,

going down toward Nothingness along my human course,
my hand entwined with yours, sweetsmiling tenderness!

So I spoke, without a word. And I saw that in the presence
of that glowing adolescence the other one was sad.

So beautiful too long, soon beautiful no more,
that woman who walked before me, watching the younger
    one.

Her beautiful strange eyes were beautiful even now
with the beauty of a flower fading as it dies.

Sotto l'aperto cielo, presso l'adolescente
come terribilmente m'apparve lo sfacelo!

Nulla fu piú sinistro che la bocca vermiglia
troppo, le tinte ciglia e l'opera del bistro

45 intorno all'occhio stanco, la piega di quei labri,
l'inganno dei cinabri sul volto troppo bianco,

gli accesi dal veleno biondissimi capelli:
in altro tempo belli d'un bel biondo sereno.

Da troppo tempo bella, non piú bella tra poco,
50 colei che vide al gioco la bimba Graziella!

– O mio cuore che valse la luce mattutina
raggiante sulla china tutte le strade false?

Cuore che non fioristi, è vano che t'affretti
verso miraggi schietti in orti meno tristi;

55 tu senti che non giova all'uomo soffermarsi,
gettare i sogni sparsi per una vita nuova.

Discenderai al Niente pel tuo sentiero umano
e non avrai per mano la dolcesorridente,

ma l'altro beveraggio avrai fino alla morte:
60 il tempo è già piú forte di tutto il tuo coraggio.

Queste pensavo cose, guidando nell'ascesa
la bicicletta accesa d'un gran mazzo di rose.

★ 15 ★

In the open light of day, with that adolescent there,
how dreadful it was to bear witness to her decay.

All the signs were ominous: the mascara-thickened lash,
the shadow she had brushed around her tired eyes,

the mouth too red and bright, the two lips like a crease,
the rouge with its deceits on the face that was too white,

the streaks that seemed to me to make her hair too blonde
that in other times had shone with a gold serenity.

So beautiful too long, soon beautiful no more,
that woman who walked before me, watching the younger
    one!

—My heart, what was the good of that sweet morning light
shining so clear and bright on all of the false roads?

Heart that has never had a flowering, why run
toward the pure mirages in those gardens much less sad?

What use is it to strive, to linger as if it mattered,
to throw away your scattered dreams for a new life?

You'll go down toward Nothingness along your human
    course
without her hand in yours, that sweetsmiling tenderness,

you'll drink another beverage until you feel death come:
already the time's become too much for all your courage.

I thought all this as, silent, I guided up the rise
the bicycle that was aflame with a rose garland.

III

Erano folti intorno gli abeti nell'assalto
dei greppi fino all'alto nevaio disadorno.

65 I greggi, sparsi a picco, in lenti beli e mugli
brucavano ai cespugli di menta il latte ricco;

e prossimi e lontani univan sonnolenti
al ritmo dei torrenti un ritmo di campani.

Lungi i pensieri foschi! Se non verrà l'amore
70 che importa? Giunge al cuore il buon odor dei boschi.

Di quali aromi opimo odore non si sa:
di resina? di timo? o di serenità?...

IV

Sostammo accanto a un prato e la Signora, china,
baciò la Signorina, ridendo nel commiato.

75 «Bada che aspetterò, che aspetteremo te;
si prende un po' di the, si cicaleccia un po'...»

«Verrò, Signora; grazie!» Dalle mie mani, in fretta,
tolse la bicicletta. E non mi disse grazie.

Non mi parlò. D'un balzo salí, prese l'avvio;
80 la macchina il fruscío ebbe d'un piede scalzo,

III

The hills were covered over with fir trees everywhere
as far as to the bare white snowfield high above.

Flocks, scattered on the hills, with soft and lowing bleats
were grazing the mint leaves and tasting their rich milk.

From far and near the flocks with the pasture's drowsy
    rhythms
tempered the louder rhythms of the currents against the rocks.

Long in somber thoughts I stood. What if love should never
    come?
Still the heart draws pleasure from the good odors of the
    wood.

From those rich aromas rising came an unknown scent to me:
scent of thyme perhaps, or resin? or perhaps serenity? . . .

IV

Then we paused along the hill, beside the pasture. The lady
bent down to kiss the young lady, laughing in farewell.

"Now we're expecting you: be sure to come visit me,
and we'll have a spot of tea, and a spot of gossip too . . ."

"I'll come, Signora, you'll see. Thank you!" And then she
    took
the bicycle quickly back. And she didn't say thank you to me.

Without a word to me, she started off with a bound,
and there was a rustling sound as of bare feet running free

d'un batter d'ali ignote, come seguita a lato
da un non so che d'alato volgente con le rote.

Restammo alle sue spalle. La strada, come un nastro
sottile d'alabastro, scendeva nella valle.

85 «Signora!... Arrivederla!...» gridò di lungi, ai venti.
Di lungi ebbero i denti un balenio di perla.

Tra la verzura folta disparve, apparve ancora.
Ancor s'udí: «...Signora!...» E fu l'ultima volta.

Grazia è scomparsa. Vola – dove? – la bicicletta...
90 «Amica, e non m'ha detta una parola sola!»

«Te ne duole?» – «Chi sa!» – «Fu taciturna, amore,
par te, come il Dolore...» – «O la Felicità...»

or the beat of unknown wings, as if there ran beside
the turning wheels some I don't know what wingéd thing.

We lingered near the pasture, watching. The road descended
to the valley like a slender ribbon of alabaster.

"Signora! . . . Goodbye! . . ." the call drifted from far away.
And even from far away her teeth were a flash of pearl.

She disappeared in the green thickness, appeared once more,
again we heard "Signora! . . ." Then all was still again.

Grazia had vanished—where?—the wheels had soared
 away . . .
"Did you notice she didn't say one word to me, my dear?"

"Are you sorry, love?"—"Who knows!"—"For you, it seems
 she was
as silent as Sorrow is . . ."—"Or silent as Happiness . . ."

Elogio degli amori ancillari

I

Allor che viene con novelle sue,
ghermir mi piace l'agile fantesca
che secretaria antica è fra noi due.

M'accende il riso della bocca fresca,
5 l'attesa vana, il motto arguto, l'ora,
e il profumo d'istoria boccaccesca...

Ella m'irride, si dibatte, implora,
invoca il nome della sua padrona:
«Ah! Che vergogna! Povera Signora!
10 Ah! Povera Signora!...» E s'abbandona.

II

Gaie figure di decamerone,
le cameriste dan, senza tormento,
piú sana voluttà che le padrone.

Non la scaltrezza del martirio lento,
15 non da morbosità polsi riarsi,
e non il tedioso sentimento

che fa le notti lunghe e i sonni scarsi,
non dopo voluttà l'anima triste:
ma un piú sereno e maschio sollazzarsi.

20 Lodo l'amore delle cameriste!

★ 21 ★

Ancillary Amours

I

I like to seize the nimble servant who
comes with her salty tales, since long ago
the trusted emissary between us two.

The laughter of her fresh mouth makes me glow,
the playful pause, the tart remark, the pout,
and the scent of a story out of Boccaccio . . .

She laughs at me, she struggles, starts to shout,
and in the name of her mistress she entreats:
"Oh, the poor lady! The shame if it gets out!

Poor lady! . . ." And she climbs between the sheets.

II

Gay figures from decamerons are these
maids who, without a load of misery,
give healthier pleasures than their mistresses.

Not the slow torture dealt so cunningly,
not the dry fevered wrists of the wretched wight,
and not the tedious sentimentality

that murders sleep and frets away the night,
not the animal that afterwards is sad:
but a more calm and masculine delight.

I celebrate the serving maids I've had!

Il gioco del silenzio

Non so se veramente fu vissuto
quel giorno della prima primavera.
Ricordo – o sogno? – un prato di velluto,
ricordo – o sogno? – un cielo che s'annera,
5 e il tuo sgomento e i lampi e la bufera
livida sul paese sconosciuto...

Poi la cascina rustica del colle
e la corsa e le grida e la massaia
e il rifugio notturno e l'ora folle
10 e te giuliva come una crestaia,
e l'aurora ed i canti in mezzo all'aia
e il ritorno in un velo di corolle...

– Parla! – Salivi per la bella strada
primaverile, tra pescheti rosa,
15 mandorli bianchi, molli di rugiada...
– Parla! – Tacevi, rigida pensosa
della cosa carpita, della cosa
che accade e non si sa mai come accada...

– Parla! – seguivo l'odorosa traccia
20 della tua gonna... Tuttavia rivedo
quel tuo sottile corpo di cinedo,
quella tua muta corrugata faccia
che par sogni l'inganno od il congedo
e che piacere a me par che le spiaccia...

The Game of Silence

I don't know if I ever really lived it
after all, that afternoon in early spring.
I recollect—or dream?—a field of velvet,
I recollect—or dream?—skies darkening,
and your fright and sheets of lightning threatening
and the storm that turned the unknown country livid . . .

Then the farmhouse on the hill and still the showers
and running and shrieking and the wife at the door
and a shelter for the night and the mad hours
and you as merry as a milliner,
and sunrise and the songs on the threshing floor
and coming back in a veil of budding flowers . . .

—Say something!—You went up where the roadway opened
in springtime loveliness between the pink
peach trees and the white almond trees, dew-softened . . .
—Say something!—You were rigid, pondering
the thing that had been stripped away, the thing
that happens and no one knows just how it happened . . .

—Say something!— I followed in the fragrantly
scented traces of your skirt . . . Yet I see still
your boyish body slight and sensual,
your muted furrowed face that seems to be
filled with its dreams of deception or farewell
and with regret for what so pleasured me . . .

25 E ancora mi negasti la tua voce
in treno. Supplicai, chino rimasi
su te, nel rombo ritmico e veloce...
Ti scossi, ti parlai con rudi frasi,
ti feci male, ti percossi quasi,
30 e ancora mi negasti la tua voce.

Giocosa amica, il Tempo vola, invola
ogni promessa. Dissipò coi baci
le tue parole tenere fugaci...
Non quel silenzio. Nel ricordo, sola
35 restò la bocca che non diè parola,
la bocca che tacendo disse: Taci!...

★ 25 ★

And still you wouldn't let me hear your voice
on the train. I stood there bending over you,
I begged in the rapid rhythm of the noise . . .
I shook you, I called you all the names I knew,
I hurt you, and I nearly struck you too,
and still you wouldn't let me hear your voice.

My playful dear, Time flies, it flies away
with every promise. With kisses I've dispelled
your every tender fleeting syllable . . .
But not that silence. Memory let stay
only that mouth that wouldn't give away
a word, that with its stillness said: Be still! . . .

Il buon compagno

Non fu l'Amore, no. Furono i sensi
curiosi di noi, nati pel culto
del sogno... E l'atto rapido, inconsulto,
ci parve fonte di misteri immensi.

5 Ma poi che nel tuo bacio ultimo spensi
l'ultimo bacio e l'ultimo sussulto,
non udii che quell'arido singulto
di te, perduta nei capelli densi.

E fu vano accostare i nostri cuori
10 già riarsi dal sogno e dal pensiero;
Amor non lega troppo eguali tempre.

Scenda l'oblio; immuni da languori
si prosegua piú forti pel sentiero,
buoni compagni ed alleati: sempre.

The Good Companion

It wasn't Love, no. It was our curious
senses, born in the worship of the dream.
Our unconsidered swiftness made it seem
a fountain of boundless mysteries to us.

In your last kiss I put out the last kiss
and the last tremor. All that I could hear,
smothered in the rich thickness of your hair
against my chest, was that dry sob of yours.

And it was futile to approach those hearts
already parched of dreams and searing thoughts.
Love never blends too equal temperaments.

Oblivion falls. Immune from lassitude
we move more strongly now along the road,
forever good companions, allies, friends.

Invernale

«... cri...i...i...i...icch»...
                               l'incrinatura
il ghiaccio rabescò, stridula e viva.
«A riva!» Ognuno guadagnò la riva
disertando la crosta malsicura.
5 «A riva! A riva!...» un soffio di paura
disperse la brigata fuggitiva.

«Resta!» Ella chiuse il mio braccio conserto,
le sue dita intrecciò, vivi legami,
alle mie dita. «Resta, se tu m'ami!»
10 E sullo specchio subdolo e deserto
soli restammo, in largo volo aperto,
ebbri d'immensità, sordi ai richiami.

Fatto lieve cosí come uno spetro,
senza passato piú, senza ricordo,
15 m'abbandonai con lei, nel folle accordo,
di larghe rote disegnando il vetro.
Dall'orlo il ghiaccio fece cricch, piú tetro...
dall'orlo il ghiaccio fece cricch, piú sordo...

Rabbrividii cosí, come chi ascolti
20 lo stridulo sogghigno della Morte,
e mi chinai, con le pupille assorte,
e trasparire vidi i nostri volti
già risupini lividi sepolti...
Dall'orlo il ghiaccio fece cricch, piú forte...

A Wintry Scene

"... cre—ee—ee—eak" ...
             in an arabesque across
the ice, shrill and alive, the crack appeared.
"Quick, to the shore!" And everybody there
broke for the shore across the trembling ice.
"Quick, to the shore! To the shore!" The revelers
were scattered by a sudden gust of fear.

"Stay!" And she held my arm against her side,
the live links of her fingers eagerly
twining with mine. "If you love me, stay with me!"
And on that empty treacherous and wide
mirror we stayed alone, in a broad free glide,
deaf to the shouting, drunk with immensity.

Light as a phantom suddenly, unbound,
no memory left, no past to recollect,
I gave myself to her in a mad compact.
Across the glass we circled round and round.
And at the edge the ice more darkly groaned . . .
and at the edge the ice more deeply cracked . . .

I shivered then, like one who hears the sound
of Death's shrill laughter. Bending, staring at
the ice, I shuddered at the sight of it:
below me two transparent faces frowned
colorless cold and laid out underground . . .
And at the edge the ice more sharply split . . .

25 Oh! Come, come, a quelle dita avvinto,
rimpiansi il mondo e la mia dolce vita!
O voce imperïosa dell'istinto!
O voluttà di vivere infinita!
Le dita liberai da quelle dita,
30 e guadagnai la ripa, ansante, vinto...

Ella sola restò, sorda al suo nome,
rotando a lungo nel suo regno solo.
Le piacque, alfine, ritoccare il suolo;
e ridendo approdò, sfatta le chiome,
35 e bella ardita palpitante come
la procellaria che raccoglie il volo.

Non curante l'affanno e le riprese
dello stuolo gaietto femminile,
mi cercò, mi raggiunse tra le file
40 degli amici con ridere cortese:
«Signor mio caro, grazie!» E mi protese
la mano breve, sibilando: – Vile! –

★ 31 ★

Caught in her fingers, how I hungered for
my sweet life and the world I lived it in!
The endless lust to live forevermore!
The imperious voice of instinct deep within!
I pulled my fingers free of hers and then,
panting, undone, I headed for the shore . . .

Alone, deaf to her name, and endlessly
revolving in her solitary reign
she stayed. At last, it pleased her to come in.
She came up laughing, she let her hair fall free,
lovely and bold and breathless she seemed to me
like a petrel safely come to earth again.

Ignoring her breathlessness and the reprimands
of all the girlish brightly colored crowd,
she looked for me, she found me, she came forward
laughingly, through the circle of my friends:
"My hero, thanks so much!" And with her hand
held out to me a moment, hissed: *"You coward!"*

L'assenza

Un bacio. Ed è lungi. Dispare
giú in fondo, là dove si perde
la strada boschiva, che pare
un gran corridoio nel verde.

5 Risalgo qui dove dianzi
vestiva il bell'abito grigio:
rivedo l'uncino, i romanzi
ed ogni sottile vestigio...

Mi piego al balcone. Abbandono
10 la gota sopra la ringhiera.
E non sono triste. Non sono
piú triste. Ritorna stasera.

E intorno declina l'estate.
E sopra un geranio vermiglio,
15 fremendo le ali caudate
si libra un enorme Papilio...

L'azzurro infinito del giorno
è come una seta ben tesa;
ma sulla serena distesa
20 la luna già pensa al ritorno.

Lo stagno risplende. Si tace
la rana. Ma guizza un bagliore
d'acceso smeraldo, di brace
azzurra: il martin pescatore...

Absence

A kiss. And she's gone. She's away
down there, where the path can't be seen
in the deep woods, still making its way
like a long corridor through the green.

I come up once more to where she
put on her gray suit. I see here
the crochet hook, the novels: I see
all the delicate traces of her . . .

I submit to the balcony door.
I abandon my cheek to the rail.
And now I'm not sad anymore.
Tonight she'll be back without fail.

And around me the summer is waning.
And with swallow-tailed wings trembling on
the tip of a bright red geranium
there hovers a huge papillon . . .

Like soft-woven silk stretched out tight
is the infinite blue afternoon:
but over the still lawn the moon
makes ready to bring back the night.

The pool is resplendent. And stilled
are the frogs. But there flashes a spear
of blue ember, bright emerald
lightning: the kingfisher's here . . .

25 E non sono triste. Ma sono
   stupito se guardo il giardino ..
   stupito di che? non mi sono
   sentito mai tanto bambino...

   Stupito di che? Delle cose.
30 I fiori mi paiono strani:
   ci sono pur sempre le rose,
   ci sono pur sempre i gerani...

And now I'm not sad. Yet I feel
so astonished to sit here and stare . . .
so astonished: I never did feel
so much like a baby before . . .

So astonished at what? What there is.
How strange all the flowers appear:
yet the roses are always here, as
the geraniums always are here . . .

Convito

I

M'è dolce cosa nel tramonto, chino
sopra gli alari dalle braci roche,
m'è dolce cosa convitar le poche
donne che mi sorrisero in cammino.

II

5 Trasumanate già, senza persone,
sorgono tutte... E quelle piú lontane,
e le compagne di speranze buone
e le piccole, ancora, e le piú vane:
mime crestaie fanti cortigiane
10 argute come in un decamerone...

Tra le faville e il crepitio dei ceppi
sorgono tutte, pallida falange...
Amore no! Amore no! Non seppi
il vero Amor per cui si ride e piange:
15 Amore non mi tanse e non mi tange;
invan m'offersi alle catene e ai ceppi.

O non amate che mi amaste, a Lui
invan proffersi il cuor che non s'appaga.
Amor non mi piagò di quella piaga
20 che mi parve dolcissima in altrui...
A quale gelo condannato fui?
Non varrà succo d'erbe o l'arte maga?

Banquet

I

To me it's sweet, bent forward to survey
the grate's hoarse embers, when the day is through,
to me it's sweet to entertain the few
women who smiled on me along my way.

II

Transhumanized already, fleshlessly
they rise . . . The little ones, and those who've gone
so far, and those who kept me company
in days of good hopes, and the vainest ones:
actresses milliners servants courtesans
all sharp with a decameron's clarity . . .

Amid the ashes and the crackling flame
they rise: a pallid phalanx reappears . . .
Not Love! Not Love! To me it never came,
true Love that brings the laughter and the tears.
Love didn't touch me, doesn't now: for years
I offered myself to the shackles, but in vain.

O unloved ones who loved me, vainly to Him
I proffered the heart unsatisfied in me.
Love didn't wound me with the wound that He
gave others and that seemed so sweet in them . . .
Into what iciness was I condemned?
Is there no help in herbs or wizardry?

III

- Un maleficio fu dalla tua culla,
né varrà l'arte maga, o sognatore!
25 Fino alla tomba il tuo gelido cuore
porterai con la tua sete fanciulla,
fanciullo triste che sapesti nulla,
ché ben sa nulla chi non sa l'amore.

Una ti bacierà con la sua bocca,
30 sforzando il chiuso cuore che resiste;
e quell'una verrà, fratello triste,
forse l'uscio picchiò con la sua nocca,
forse alle spalle già ti sta, ti tocca;
già ti cinge di sue chiome non viste...

35 Si dilegua con occhi di sorella
indi ciascuna. E si riprende il cuore.

«Fratello triste, cui mentí l'Amore,
che non ti menta l'altra cosa bella!»

III

—Dreamer, from the cradle you were cursed,
and there's no help that wizardry can bring!
All the way to the tomb you'll go wandering,
bearing your icy heart and your infant thirst,
sad infant who knew nothing from the first:
who knows not love cannot know anything.

Still, one will kiss you, forcing her way into
the fastened heart that doesn't want her there.
Sad brother, she will find you anywhere:
perhaps she's given the door a tap or two,
perhaps she's already beside you, touching you,
already encircling you with her unseen hair . . .

Then each one evanesces, with the eyes
of a sister. And the heart's restored, at rest.

"Love's lied to you, sad brother. It were best
that the other beautiful thing not tell you lies!"

II

On the Threshold

☆

Alle soglie

Alle soglie

I

Mio cuore, monello giocondo che ride pur anco nel pianto,
mio cuore, bambino che è tanto felice d'esistere al mondo,

pur chiuso nella tua nicchia, ti pare sentire di fuori
sovente qualcuno che picchia, che picchia... Sono i dottori.

5 Mi picchiano in vario lor metro spiando non so quali segni,
m'auscultano con li ordegni il petto davanti e di dietro.

E senton chi sa quali tarli i vecchi saputi... A che scopo?
Sorriderei quasi, se dopo non bisognasse pagarli...

«Appena un lieve sussurro all'apice... qui... la clavicola...»
10 E con la matita ridicola disegnano un circolo azzurro.

«Nutrirsi... non fare piú versi... nessuna notte piú insonne...
non piú sigarette... non donne... tentare bei cieli piú tersi:

On the Threshold

I

My heart, such a merry young child who laughs as his own
    teardrops fall,
my heart, still a boy after all, so happy to be in the world,

secure in your niche—but what's that? It seems you hear
    somebody tapping:
from outside comes a rat-a-tat-tat, rat-a-tat . . . It's the
    medicos rapping.

They thump me in varying meters: with all of the tools of
    their craft
they auscultate me fore and aft—who knows what they're
    after, the bleeders?

The old know-it-alls sense the wending of who knows what
    worms in their traces.
And for what? I could laugh in their faces, if not for the bill
    they'll be sending.

"A tiny susurrus comes through at the apex . . . the
    clavicle . . . here . . ."
And the ludicrous crayons appear, and they draw a bright
    circle of blue.

"Eat up . . . no more making of rhymes . . . no more staying
    up nights . . . no brunettes
and no blondes . . . no more cigarettes . . . try to get to some
    sunnier climes:

Nervi... Rapallo... San Remo... cacciare la malinconia;
e se permette faremo qualche radioscopia...»

II

15 O cuore non forse che avvisi solcarti, con grande paura,
la casa ben chiusa ed oscura, di gelidi raggi improvvisi?

Un fluido investe il torace, frugando il men peggio e il
   peggiore,
trascorre, e senza dolore disegna su sfondo di brace

e l'ossa e gli organi grami, al modo che un lampo nel
   fosco
20 disegna il profilo d'un bosco, coi minimi intrichi dei
   rami.

E vedon chi sa quali tarli i vecchi saputi... A che scopo?
Sorriderei quasi, se dopo non fosse mestieri pagarli.

III

Mio cuore, monello giocondo che ride pur anco nel
   pianto,
mio cuore, bambino che è tanto felice d'esistere al
   mondo,

Nervi . . . San Remo . . . Rapallo . . . cast away melancholy,
   don't mope.
And if you'll permit, now we'll follow by using the
   radioscope."

II

O heart, as you happen to gaze, don't you see with a shudder
   of fright
the house that was dark and shut tight invaded by sudden
   cold rays?

Through my thorax a fluid unrolls, through the less malign
   and the malign,
without sorrow it starts to design on a background of hot
   glowing coals

all the pitiful organs, the bones, like lightning across a dark
   night
outlining a forest with tight tiny branches and twigs
   overgrown.

The old know-it-alls watch the playing of who knows what
   worms in their traces.
And for what? I could laugh in their faces, if not for the bill
   I'll be paying.

III

My heart, such a merry young child who laughs as his own
   teardrops fall,
my heart, still a boy after all, so happy to be in the world,

25 mio cuore dubito forte – ma per te solo m'accora –
che venga quella Signora dall'uomo detta la Morte.

(Dall'uomo: ché l'acqua la pietra l'erba l'insetto l'aedo
le danno un nome, che, credo, esprima una cosa non tetra).

È una Signora vestita di nulla e che non ha forma.
30 Protende su tutto le dita, e tutto che tocca trasforma.

Tu senti un benessere come un incubo senza dolori;
ti svegli mutato di fuori, nel volto nel pelo nel nome.

Ti svegli dagl'incubi innocui, diverso ti senti, lontano;
né piú ti ricordi i colloqui tenuti con guidogozzano.

35 Or taci nel petto corroso, mio cuore! Io resto al supplizio,
sereno come uno sposo e placido come un novizio.

my heart, now I feel a great fear—but it's only for you I'm
  concerned—
that the Lady that humans have learned to call Death will
  quite shortly appear.

(Only humans: the water the bird the insect the rock and the
  bard
all call her a name that's less hard, all use a less desolate
  word.)

She's a Lady who dresses in nothing, who hasn't a substance
  or form:
hands stretched out, she overlooks nothing, all she touches
  she'll quickly transform.

You'll feel peacefulness seep through your frame like a
  nightmare that captures you sweetly,
you'll wake with your self changed completely, in face and in
  hair and in name.

You'll wake from soft nightmares in peace, you'll feel
  yourself other, and gone now,
you'll no more recall colloquies with a creature called
  guidogozzano.

Be still in this gnawed-away chest, o my heart: I lie suffering
  now
serene as a bridegroom, at rest like a novice approaching the
  vow.

Il più atto

Adolescente forte, quadre le spalle e il busto,
irride al mio tramonto con chiari occhi sereni;
sdegna i pensieri torpidi, gli studi vani, i freni;
tempra in cimenti rudi il bel corpo robusto.

5 Il ramo è che rallevi già sullo stesso fusto
accanto al ramo spoglio, Morte che sopravvieni...
A lui vada la vita! A lui le rose, i beni,
le donne ed i piaceri! Madre Natura, è giusto.

Ed egli sia quell'uno felice ch'io non fui!
10 Questa speranza sola m'addolcirà lo strazio
del Nulla... Sulle soglie del Tempo e dello Spazio
è pur dolce conforto rivivere in altrui.

Senza querele, o Morte, discendo ai regni bui;
di ciò che tu mi desti, o Vita, io ti ringrazio.
15 Sorrido al mio fratello... Poi, rassegnato e sazio,
a lui cedo la coppa. E già mi sento lui.

The Fittest

A sturdy adolescent, square shoulders and deep chest,
with clear and steady eyes he mocks me as I wane.
He scorns the torpid thoughts, the studies vain, the reins.
His handsome body hardens through every heavy test.

The branch already feeds on the same trunk, abreast
of the barren branch that droops where Death already reigns.
To him goes life! To him the roses and the gains,
the women and the good times! Mother Nature knows best.

And he will be the happy one I've never been!
That single hope is all that sweetens my decline
to Nothing . . . On the threshold of Time and Space I find
sweet comfort to think we live in others once again.

Without a quibble, Death, I go down to your dark realm,
and Life, I give you thanks for all that once was mine.
I smile at my brother . . . And then, sated and resigned,
to him I pass the cup. And already I stir in him.

Salvezza

Vivere cinque ore?
Vivere cinque età?...
Benedetto il sopore
che m'addormenterà...

5 Ho goduto il risveglio
dell'anima leggiera:
meglio dormire, meglio
prima della mia sera.

Poi che non ha ritorno
10 il riso mattutino.
La bellezza del giorno
è tutta nel mattino.

Salvation

To live for just five hours?
To live five centuries? . . .
Blest drowsiness whose powers
will carry me to peace . . .

The awakening, the leaping
when soul was light and clear:
better to be sleeping
before my evening's here.

When the morning's ended
day's laughter is all done.
Day's loveliness is splendid
only in the morning sun.

Paolo e Virginia

I figli dell'infortunio

> Amanti, miserere
> miserere di questa mia giocosa
> aridità larvata di chimere!

I

Io fui Paolo già. Troppo mi scuote
il nome di Virginia. Ebbro e commosso
leggo il volume senza fine amaro;
chino su quelle pagine remote
5 rivivo tempi già vissuti e posso
piangere (ancora!) come uno scolaro...
Splende nel sogno chiaro
l'isola dove nacqui e dove amai;
rivedo gli orizzonti immaginari
10 e favolosi come gli scenari,
la rada calma dove i marinai
trafficavano spezie e legni rari...
Virginia ride al limite del bosco
e trepida saluta...
15 Risorge chiara dal passato fosco
la patria perduta
che non conobbi mai, che riconosco...

II

O soave contrada! O palme somme
erette verso il cielo come dardi,
20 flabelli verdi sibilanti ai venti!
Alberi delle manne e delle gomme,

Paul and Virginia

The children of misfortune

> *Lovers, pity me,*
> *pity this grinning dust, be merciful*
> *to this croaking ghost wrapped in a fantasy!*

I

I was already Paul. I am too taken
by Virginia's name. Intoxicated, moved,
I read the volume bitter without end.
Bent over the distant pages I reawaken
and live once more a time already lived,
and I can weep a schoolboy's tears again . . .
And in a clear dream then
shines the bright island where I was in love,
where I was born: and once again I see
as fabulous as painted scenery
the imaginary horizons, the quiet cove
where the sailors traded spice and ivory . . .
Virginia walks by the woods with laughing eyes,
she smiles and waves her hand . . .
Out of the dark past I see it rise
clearly, the vanished land
I never knew, the land I recognize . . .

II

The gentle latitudes, the arching palms
like arrows pointing to the sky, the breeze
that whispers through the fanlike leaves, the tall
trees of manna and the trees of gum,

ebani cupi, sandali gagliardi,
liane contorte, felci arborescenti!
Virginia, ti rammenti
25 di quella sempiterna primavera?
Rammenti i campi d'indaco e di the,
e le Missioni e il Padre e il Vicerè,
quel Tropico rammenti, di maniera,
un poco falso, come piace a me?...
30 Ti rammenti il colore
del Settecento esotico, l'odore
di pace, filtro di non so che frutto
e di non so che fiore,
il filtro che dismemora di tutto?...

III

35 Ti chiamavo sorella, mi chiamavi
fratello. Tutto favoriva intorno
le nostre adolescenze ignare e belle.
Era la vita semplice degli avi,
la vita delle origini, il Ritorno
40 sognato da Gian Giacomo ribelle.
Di tutto ignari: delle
Scienze e dell'Indagine che prostra
e della Storia, favola mentita,
abitavamo l'isola romita
45 senz'altro dove che la terra nostra
senz'altro quando che la nostra vita.
Le dolci madri a sera
c'insegnavano il Bene, la Pietà,
la Fede unica e vera;
50 e lenti innalzavamo la preghiera
al Padre Nostro che nei cieli sta...

the arborescent ferns, dark ebonies,
strong sandalwoods, and vines that twist and crawl:
Virginia, do you recall
that sempiternal spring, where nothing changed?
Recall the fields of tea, of indigo,
the Father and the Viceroy, and that slow
Tropic so artistically arranged,
a little false (and I preferred it so)? . . .
Do you recall the tint
of the exotic eighteenth century, the scent
of peace, a philter of I don't know what fruit
and I don't know what plant,
blurring every remembrance with its root? . . .

III

I called you sister and you called me brother.
Nourished by all our island had to give,
our youth was lovely and was ignorant.
We lived the simple life with one another,
the life of the birds, the life of the Primitive
that Jean-Jacques dreamed of in his discontent.
And we were ignorant
of Science and of stunting Inquiry,
of History, that lying fairy tale.
We lived upon our solitary isle
without a where beyond what we could see,
without a when beyond what we could feel.
And when the day was done
our two sweet mothers taught the Good, the leaven
of Mercy, and the one
true Faith: and slowly and in unison
we raised the prayer to Our Father who art in heaven . . .

IV

    Seduti in coro, nelle sere calme,
    seguivamo i piròfori che ardeano
    nella verzura dell'Eremitaggio;
55 fra i dolci intercolunni delle palme
    scintillava la Luna sull'oceano,
    giungeva un canto flebile e selvaggio...
    Tra noi sedeva il Saggio
    e ci ammoniva con forbiti esempi
60 ispirati da Omero e da Virgilio...
    L'isola si chiamò per suo consiglio
    secondo la retorica dei tempi:
    Rivo dell'Amistà, Colle del Giglio,
    Fonte dei Casti Accenti...
65 Era il tempo dei Nestori morali,
    dei *saggi ammonimenti*,
    era il tempo dei *buoni sentimenti*,
    della *virtú*, dei *semplici ideali*.

V

    Immuni dalla gara che divampa
70 nel triste mondo, crescevamo paghi
    dei beni della rete e della freccia;
    belli e felici come in una stampa
    del tuo romanzo, correvamo i laghi
    nella svelta piroga di corteccia;
75 sull'ora boschereccia
    numeravamo l'ora il giorno l'anno:
    – Quant'anni avrete poi? – Quanti n'avranno
    quei due palmizi dispari, alle soglie... –
    – Verrete? – Quando i manghi fioriranno... –

IV

Sitting together in the quiet shade
at dusk, we watched the fireflies merrily
blinking along the green of our retreat.
Between the palm trees' double colonnade
we watched the moonlight sparkling on the sea,
we heard the plaintive singing, wild and sweet . . .
We sat there at the feet
of the Sage who counseled us with many a page
of Homer and Virgil, many a smooth reflection . . .
We named the island, after his direction,
according to the rhetoric of the age:
the Hill of Lilies, the Current of Affection,
the Fountain of Pure Accents . . .
It was the age of Nestors, of high appeals
and wise admonishments,
it was the age of tender sentiments,
the age of virtue and of plain ideals.

V

Immune from all the striving and the craving
of the sad world, we grew up satisfied
with the harvest of the net and arrow. True
and happy as ourselves in an engraving
in your romantic tale, we used to glide
along the lakes in a swift bark canoe.
By the living world we knew
the passing of the hour the day the year:
—How old are you? —As old as the smaller one
of the palm trees growing on the threshold here . . .
—You'll come? —When the mangoes ripen in the sun . . .

80 – Sorella, già si chiudono le foglie,
trema la prima stella...
– Il sicomoro ha l'ombra alle radici:
è mezzodí, sorella... –
Era la nostra vita come quella
85 dei Fauni e delle Driadi felici.

VI

Ma giunse l'ora che non ha conforto.
Seco ti volle nei suoi feudi vasti
la zia di Francia, perfida in vedetta.
Il Viceré ti fece trarre al porto
90 dalle sue genti barbare! E lasciasti
lacrimando la terra benedetta,
ogni cosa diletta
piú caramente, per la nave errante!
Solo, malcerto della mia sciagura,
95 vissi coi negri e le due madri affrante;
ti chiamavo; nei sassi e nelle piante
rivedevo la tua bianca figura
che non avrei rivista...
E volse l'anno disperato... Un giorno
100 il buon Padre Battista
annunciò la tua fuga e il tuo ritorno,
ed una nave, il San Germano, in vista!

VII

Folle di gioia, con le madri in festa,
scesi alla rada: – Giunge la mia sposa,
105 ritorna a me Virginia mia fedele!... –

—The shadow's on the sycamore's roots, my dear
sister, the morning hours
are gone . . . —Already all the leaves and flowers
are closing: the light is gone,
sister, I see the first star gleaming . . .— Ours
was the happy life of the Dryads and the Fauns.

VI

But came the day of disillusionment.
There was a letter summoning you to stay
in France with your wealthy aunt, alert to sting.
The Viceroy came with his barbarous regiment
to drag you off to the ship. You went away
weeping from the land of blessed spring,
from every well-loved thing,
to sail for France upon the wandering sea.
Shapeless in my wretchedness, alone,
I lived with the broken mothers in misery,
with the blacks. I called you. I saw what couldn't be:
in every flower and in every stone
I saw your clear white shape . . .
The dead year turned. Another year began . . .
One day that good old man
Father Baptiste brought news of your escape,
and of your return—today!—on the *Saint-Geran*!

VII

Mad with delight, I hastened arm in arm
with our two mothers to the cove: —My bride,
my faithful Virginia is coming home to me! . . .—

Or ecco sollevarsi la Tempesta,
una tempesta bella e artificiosa
come il Diluvio delle vecchie tele.
Appaiono le vele
110 del San Germano al balenar frequente,
stridono procellarie gemebonde,
albàtri cupi. Il mare si confonde
col cielo apocalittico. La gente
guata la nave tra il furor dell'onde.
115 Tutto l'Oceano Indiano
ribolle spaventoso, ulula, scroscia,
ma sul fragore s'alza un grido umano
terribile d'angoscia:
— Virginia è là! Salvate il San Germano!... —

VIII

120 Il San Germano affonda. I marinai
tentano indarno il salvataggio. Tutti
balzano in mare, da che vana è l'arte.
Rotto ha la nave contro i polipai,
sovra coperta già fremono i flutti,
125 spezza il vento governi alberi sarte...
Virginia ecco in disparte
pallida e sola!... Un marinaio nudo
tenta svestirla e seco darsi all'onda;
si rifiuta Virginia pudibonda
130 (retorica del tempo!) e si fa scudo
delle due mani... Il San Germano affonda;
il San Germano affonda... Un sciabordare
ultimo, cupo, mozzo:
e non rivedo al chiaro balenare
135 la nave!... Il mio singhiozzo
disperde il vasto singhiozzar del mare.

Then suddenly the rising of the Storm,
as artificial and as prettified
as the Flood in some old oil or tapestry.
The topsails suddenly
coupled with the lightning flashing down,
while overhead the moaning petrels thrashed,
and the sullen albatross. The dark sea flashed
and bled into the screaming sky. The town
all stared in horror as the ship was smashed
by the raving sea. The entire Indian
Ocean was boiling, roaring, howling—and then
there rises a terrible howling human cry
shrieking above the din:
—Virginia's on that ship! Don't let her die! . . .—

VIII

The *Saint-Geran* goes down. The sailors try
in vain to save it. Driven from the wreck
they leap into the sea. The waves prevail,
the ship is broken on the reefs, the high
billows already wash across the deck,
the wind dismantles rudder mast and sail . . .
Virginia is at the rail,
pale and alone! . . . Now a naked sailor stands
beside her trying to strip away her gown
to save her: in her purity she sinks down
(the rhetoric of the age!) with her two hands
clasped in a shield . . . The *Saint-Geran* goes down,
the *Saint-Geran* goes down . . . Now finally
it founders, shudders, throbs:
in the brilliant lightning I no longer see
the ship! . . . And then my sobs
scatter the boundless sobbing of the sea.

IX

Era l'alba e il tuo bel corpo travolto
stava tra l'alghe e le meduse attorte,
placido come in placido sopore.
140 Muto mi reclinai sopra quel volto
dove già le viole della morte
mescevansi alle rose del pudore...
Disperato dolore!
Dolore senza grido e senza pianto!
145 Morta giacevi col tuo sogno intatto,
tornavi morta a chi t'amava tanto!
Nella destra chiudevi il mio ritratto,
con la manca premevi il cuore infranto...
– Virginia! O sogni miei!
150 Virginia! – E ti chiamai, con occhi fissi...
– Virginia! Amore che ritorni e sei
la Morte! Amore... Morte... – E piú non dissi.

X

Morii d'amore. Oggi rinacqui e vivo,
ma piú non amo. Il mio sogno è distrutto
155 per sempre e il cuore non fiorisce piú.
E chiamo invano Amore fuggitivo,
invano piange questa Musa a lutto
che porta il lutto a tutto ciò che fu.
Il mio cuore è laggiú,
160 morto con te, nell'isola fiorente,
dove i palmizi gemono sommessi
lungo la Baia della Fede Ardente...
Ah! Se potessi amare! Ah! Se potessi
amare, canterei sí novamente!
165 Ma l'anima corrosa

IX

Dawn, and your lovely corpse lay on the shore,
there with the slugs and seaweed in the sun,
peaceful as in a peaceful drowsiness.
Silent I looked down on that face once more
where the violets of death already had begun
to darken the rose of purity . . . Spiritless,
in a grief of hopelessness,
without a cry, without a tear to flow.
Dead you lay there with your dream intact,
you came home dead to the one who loved you so.
Your left hand pressed the heart that had been cracked,
your right hand clasped my face in cameo . . .
—Virginia! O my dreams!
Virginia!— Eyes riveted, I stood on the shore . . .
—Virginia! Beloved come home to the quiet streams
in Death! Beloved . . . Death . . .— And I said no more.

X

I died for love. Reborn today, I live
but I don't love. The dream is dead, the heart
is a stony ground where flowers never grow.
Vainly I call the beloved fugitive,
in vain the mourning Muse puts on its art,
mourning for everything it used to know.
My heart is down below,
dead with you, buried in the flower-blown
island we used to love, along the Bay
of Ardent Faith, where the palm trees softly moan . . .
If I could love, if I could love today,
what bright new songs! Instead I sit alone,
and the corroded soul

sogghigna nelle sue gelide sere...
Amanti! Miserere,
miserere di questa mia giocosa
aridità larvata di chimere!

sits in the cold night sneering frigidly . . .
Lovers! Pity me,
pity this grinning dust, be merciful
to this croaking ghost wrapped in a fantasy!

La signorina Felicita

ovvero La Felicità

10 luglio: Santa Felicita

I

Signorina Felicita, a quest'ora
scende la sera nel giardino antico
della tua casa. Nel mio cuore amico
scende il ricordo. E ti rivedo ancora,
5 e Ivrea rivedo e la cerulea Dora
e quel dolce paese che non dico.

Signorina Felicita, è il tuo giorno!
A quest'ora che fai? Tosti il caffè,
e il buon aroma si diffonde intorno?
10 O cuci i lini e canti e pensi a me,
all'avvocato che non fa ritorno?
E l'avvocato è qui: che pensa a te.

Pensa i bei giorni d'un autunno addietro,
Vill'Amarena a sommo dell'ascesa
15 coi suoi ciliegi e con la sua Marchesa
dannata, e l'orto dal profumo tetro
di busso e i cocci innumeri di vetro
sulla cinta vetusta, alla difesa...

Vill'Amarena! Dolce la tua casa
20 in quella grande pace settembrina!
La tua casa che veste una cortina
di granoturco fino alla cimasa:
come una dama secentista, invasa
dal Tempo, che vestí da contadina.

Signorina Felicita

or Felicity

July 10: Saint Felicita

I

Signorina Felicita, the evening hour
descends in the old garden of your home.
Into this friendly heart of mine there come
descending memories. I see you once more,
I see Ivrea once more and the blue Dora
and that sweet countryside that I don't name.

Signorina Felicita, today is your
name day. What are you doing now? Are you
roasting the coffee as rich aromas pour?
Or mending the linen and singing, and thinking too
of the lawyer who doesn't come back anymore?
Here is the lawyer: and he thinks of you.

He thinks of the bright days of a lost fall,
Vill'Amarena at the crest of the hill
with its cherry trees and with its pitiful
doomed Marchesa, and the gloomy pall
of the boxwood orchard and the crumbling wall
with its bits of broken glass, defending still . . .

Vill'Amarena under a country sky
in all that wide September peacefulness,
a curtain of cornstalks all around the house
reaching up to the rooftops, like a high
seventeenth-century lady invaded by
Time, who took to wearing peasant dress.

25 Bell'edificio triste inabitato!
Grate panciute, logore, contorte!
Silenzio! Fuga delle stanze morte!
Odore d'ombra! Odore di passato!
Odore d'abbandono desolato!
30 Fiabe defunte delle sovrapporte!

Ercole furibondo ed il Centauro,
le gesta dell'eroe navigatore,
Fetonte e il Po, lo sventurato amore
d'Arianna, Minosse, il Minotauro,
35 Dafne rincorsa, trasmutata in lauro
tra le braccia del Nume ghermitore...

Penso l'arredo – che malinconia! –
penso l'arredo squallido e severo,
antico e nuovo: la pirografia
40 sui divani corinzi dell'Impero,
la cartolina della Bella Otero
alle specchiere... Che malinconia!

Antica suppellettile forbita!
Armadi immensi pieni di lenzuola
45 che tu rammendi paziente... Avita
semplicità che l'anima consola,
semplicità dove tu vivi sola
con tuo padre la tua semplice vita!

II

Quel tuo buon padre – in fama d'usuraio –
50 quasi bifolco, m'accoglieva senza
inquietarsi della mia frequenza,

The empty mansion sad and beautiful,
the bellied gratings bent and rusted, floors
of dead rooms and of silent corridors,
odor of shadows and the past, the still
odor of abandonment and chill,
the faded legends carved above the doors.

Hercules in his fury and the Centaur,
the exploits of the wanderer on the sea,
Phaethon and the Po, the misery
of Ariadne, Minos, the Minotaur,
Daphne pursued and changed forevermore,
in the arms of the clutching god, to a laurel tree . . .

I think of the furniture—what melancholy—
I think of the furniture austere and mean,
old and new: Empire sofas with frilly
Corinthian designs burned in the grain,
the postcard of La Belle Otero in
the frame of the looking glass . . . What melancholy . . .

The old and fiercely polished furnishings,
huge cabinets piled with sheets that patiently
you mend . . . An ancient heritage that brings
the consolations of simplicity
to the soul, where in your father's company
you live the simple life of simple things.

II

Your good old father—a usurer, they said—
almost a hayseed, never took offense
at all my calls. He'd greet me, and commence

mi parlava dell'uve e del massaio,
mi confidava certo antico guaio
notarile, con somma deferenza.

55 «Senta, avvocato...» e mi traeva inqueto
nel salone, talvolta, con un atto
che leggeva lentissimo, in segreto.
Io l'ascoltavo docile, distratto
da quell'odor d'inchiostro putrefatto,
60 da quel disegno strano del tappeto,

da quel salone buio e troppo vasto...
«... la Marchesa fuggí... Le spese cieche...»
da quel parato a ghirlandette, a greche...
«dell'ottocento e dieci, ma il catasto...»
65 da quel tic-tac dell'orologio guasto...
«... l'ipotecario è morto, e l'ipoteche...»

Capiva poi che non capivo niente
e sbigottiva: «Ma l'ipotecario
è morto, è morto!!...» – «E se l'ipotecario
70 è morto, allora...» Fortunatamente
tu comparivi tutta sorridente:
«Ecco il nostro malato immaginario!»

III

Sei quasi brutta, priva di lusinga
nelle tue vesti quasi campagnole,
75 ma la tua faccia buona e casalinga,
ma i bei capelli di color di sole,
attorti in minutissime trecciuole,
ti fanno un tipo di beltà fiamminga...

to talk about all the grapes he'd harvested,
to tell me about the woe that filled his head
on a point of law, with the height of deference.

"Say, counselor . . ." And, upset, he'd shepherd me
into the parlor sometimes, where he'd read
ever so slowly, almost secretly,
a deed. I'd listen, letting distractions breed:
the odor of ink decaying on the deed,
the odd design of the carpet's tracery,

the outsized parlor deepening into brown . . .
". . . the Marchesa ran away . . . she'd spent it as . . ."
the curtains garlanded like a Greek vase . . .
"from 1810, but the tax-rolls in the town . . ."
the tick-tock of the old clock running down . . .
". . . the mortgage holder's dead, and the mortgages . . ."

Until at last he saw that I could see
nothing: "But the mortgage holder's dead,
he's dead, I tell you!"—"The mortgage holder's dead?
Well then, in that case . . ." Just then, fortunately
you walked in all in smiles and said to me:
"Here's our imaginary invalid!"

III

You're almost ugly, unvoluptuous
in near-peasant clothes from country woollen spun,
and yet with the domestic wholesomeness
of your good face, and with your fine hair done
in tight braids, hair the color of the sun,
you have a kind of Flemish loveliness . . .

E rivedo la tua bocca vermiglia
80 cosí larga nel ridere e nel bere,
e il volto quadro, senza sopracciglia,
tutto sparso d'efelidi leggiere
e gli occhi fermi, l'iridi sincere
azzurre d'un azzurro di stoviglia...

85 Tu m'hai amato. Nei begli occhi fermi
rideva una blandizie femminina.
Tu civettavi con sottili schermi,
tu volevi piacermi, Signorina:
e piú d'ogni conquista cittadina
90 mi lusingò quel tuo voler piacermi!

Ogni giorno salivo alla tua volta
pel soleggiato ripido sentiero.
Il farmacista non pensò davvero
un'amicizia cosí bene accolta,
95 quando ti presentò la prima volta
l'ignoto villeggiante forestiero.

Talora – già la mensa era imbandita –
mi trattenevi a cena. Era una cena
d'altri tempi, col gatto e la falena
100 e la stoviglia semplice e fiorita
e il commento dei cibi e Maddalena
decrepita, e la siesta e la partita...

Per la partita, verso ventun'ore
giungeva tutto l'inclito collegio
105 politico locale: il molto Regio
Notaio, il signor Sindaco, il Dottore;
ma – poiché trasognato giocatore –
quei signori m'avevano in dispregio...

And I can see your bright red mouth again
(when you laughed or when you drank, how wide it grew),
your square face with no eyebrows and a thin
sprinkle of light freckles, and those two
bright steady eyes of yours, as pure and blue
as pots and dishes of blue porcelain . . .

You loved me. Those two steady eyes of yours
were sparkling with a feminine blandishment.
You flirted with me with your slender lures,
you wished to please me: Signorina, it meant
more than all city conquests to catch a hint
of the wish to please me in those eyes of yours.

Every day I used to climb toward you
along the sunlit pathway, up the rise.
How little did the pharmacist surmise
the friendship that would grow between us two,
that first time when he introduced you to
the stranger vacationing under country skies.

The table was set already when I came.
You'd ask me to stay to dinner, and we'd eat
a dinner from another time, complete
with cat, moths, simple flowered dishes, lame
old Maddalena, comments on the meat,
a siesta, and then later on the game . . .

At game time, around nine, the house grew gayer
with the whole illustrious local political
committee in full cry: the very Royal
Notary, the Doctor, his honor the Mayor.
But with the cards I was a dreamy player,
and all those worthies thought I was a fool . . .

M'era piú dolce starmene in cucina
110 tra le stoviglie a vividi colori:
tu tacevi, tacevo, Signorina:
godevo quel silenzio e quegli odori
tanto tanto per me consolatori,
di basilico d'aglio di cedrina...

115 Maddalena con sordo brontolio
disponeva gli arredi ben detersi,
rigovernava lentamente ed io,
già smarrito nei sogni piú diversi,
accordavo le sillabe dei versi
120 sul ritmo eguale dell'acciotolio.

Sotto l'immensa cappa del camino
(in me rivive l'anima d'un cuoco
forse...) godevo il sibilo del fuoco;
la canzone d'un grillo canterino
125 mi diceva parole, a poco a poco,
e vedevo Pinocchio e il mio destino...

Vedevo questa vita che m'avanza:
chiudevo gli occhi nei presagi grevi;
aprivo gli occhi: tu mi sorridevi,
130 ed ecco rifioriva la speranza!

Giungevano le risa, i motti brevi
dei giocatori, da quell'altra stanza.

IV

Bellezza riposata dei solai
dove il rifiuto secolare dorme!
135 In quella tomba, tra le vane forme

The kitchen was where I preferred to be,
among the brightly colored dishes. You
sat silently, and I sat silently
enjoying the quiet and the odors too,
the basil, garlic, citron, warming to
the consolations that they offered me . . .

Maddalena with her grumbling patter
scrubbed the dishes till they all were gleaming,
washing them slowly, keeping up her chatter,
while I, already lost in scattered dreaming,
tuned the syllables of the verses streaming
in time to the steady rhythm of the clatter.

Under the chimney cowl (I calculate
the soul of a cook is reborn in me) I'd listen
to the hissing fire, with no higher ambition.
There was a singing cricket on the grate:
little by little he chirped his admonition,
and I could see Pinocchio and my fate . . .

I saw the rest of my life in a flash of doom:
I closed my eyes with a grave prophecy.
I opened my eyes again: you smiled at me,
and once more hope was suddenly in bloom!

Loud barks of laughter and quick repartee
came from the players in the other room.

IV

The attic in sublime tranquility
where the refuse of the centuries lay asleep.
There in that tomb, amid every empty shape

di ciò ch'è stato e non sarà piú mai,
bianca bella cosí che sussultai,
la Dama apparve nella tela enorme:

«È quella che lasciò, per infortuni,
140 la casa al nonno di mio nonno... E noi
la confinammo nel solaio, poi
che porta pena... L'han veduta alcuni
lasciare il quadro; in certi noviluni
s'ode il suo passo lungo i corridoi...»

145 Il nostro passo diffondeva l'eco
tra quei rottami del passato vano,
e la Marchesa dal profilo greco,
altocinta, l'un piede ignudo in mano,
si riposava all'ombra d'uno speco
150 arcade, sotto un bel cielo pagano.

Intorno a quella che rideva illusa
nel ricco peplo, e che morí di fame,
v'era una stirpe logora e confusa:
topaie, materassi, vasellame,
155 lucerne, ceste, mobili: ciarpame
reietto, cosí caro alla mia Musa!

Tra i materassi logori e le ceste
v'erano stampe di persone egregie;
incoronato delle frondi regie
160 v'era *Torquato nei giardini d'Este.*
«Avvocato, perché su quelle teste
buffe si vede un ramo di ciliegie?»

Io risi, tanto che fermammo il passo,
e ridendo pensai questo pensiero:
165 Oimè! La Gloria! un corridoio basso,

of things that were and never more will be,
so white and lovely that she startled me,
the Lady appeared on a canvas broad and deep:

"When things went bad, she left the villa to
my grandfather's grandfather . . . The pain she bore,
we couldn't bear to look at her anymore . . .
She leaves the picture, people have seen her too.
Sometimes at midnight, when the moon is new,
we hear her footsteps in the corridor . . ."

Our footsteps scattered echoes through the pile
of wreckage from the empty days gone by
while the Marchesa with her Greek profile,
one bare foot in her hand, waist belted high,
sat by the grotto of an Arcadian isle,
tranquil under a lovely pagan sky.

Round her who laughed in that airy atmosphere
in her rich peplum, and who starved to death,
there lay a bewildering jumble: a chandelier,
mattresses, crockery, a few rats' nests,
hampers, old furniture, and all the rest
of the faded rubbish that my Muse holds dear.

Engravings of the eminent were staring
among the hampers and the wornout beds.
Torquato in the Este Gardens stood
crowned in the royal bays, with noble bearing.
"Counselor, why are all those people wearing
those cherry branches on their silly heads?"

I laughed so hard I couldn't walk anymore,
and as I stood there laughing, a thought came:
Alas for Glory—a low corridor,

tre ceste, un canterano dell'Impero,
la brutta effigie incorniciata in nero
e sotto il nome di Torquato Tasso!

Allora, quasi a voce che richiama,
170 esplorai la pianura autunnale
dall'abbaino secentista, ovale,
a telaietti fitti, ove la trama
del vetro deformava il panorama
come un antico smalto innaturale.

175 Non vero (e bello) come in uno smalto
a zone quadre, apparve il Canavese:
Ivrea turrita, i colli di Montalto,
la Serra dritta, gli alberi, le chiese;
e il mio sogno di pace si protese
180 da quel rifugio luminoso ed alto.

Ecco – pensavo – questa è l'Amarena,
ma laggiú, oltre i colli dilettosi,
c'è il Mondo: quella cosa tutta piena
di lotte e di commerci turbinosi,
185 la cosa tutta piena di quei «cosi
con due gambe» che fanno tanta pena...

L'Eguagliatrice numera le fosse,
ma quelli vanno, spinti da chimere
vane, divisi e suddivisi a schiere
190 opposte, intesi all'odio e alle percosse:
cosí come ci son formiche rosse,
cosí come ci son formiche nere...

Schierati al sole o all'ombra della Croce,
tutti travolge il turbine dell'oro;
195 o Musa – oimè! – che può giovare loro

an ugly effigy in a great black frame,
a little plate with Torquato Tasso's name,
three hampers, and an Empire chest of drawers.

And then, as to a voice that summoned me,
I turned to gaze out at the autumn plain
refracted in each closely fitted pane,
where, filtered through the seventeenth-century
window, the panorama seemed to be
an old enamel done in a stylized vein.

Unreal (and beautiful) as in the bright
squares of enamel appeared the Canavese:
Ivrea's turrets, Montalto's hills, upright
Mount Serra, all the churches and the trees.
And slowly I stretched out my dream of peace
down from the shelter of that lustrous height.

This is the Amarena, but down there—
I stood there thinking—out beyond the range
of the delectable hills, is a mad affair
of struggle and whirling trade and eternal change
they call the World: a thing filled up with strange
"two-legged things" that spread pain everywhere . . .

The Equalizer counts the coffins out,
but on they go on their shadowy battleground,
divided and subdivided in hidebound
masses, all intent on hate and rout:
like so many red ants they run about,
like so many black ants they run around . . .

Massed in the sun or the shadow of the Cross,
the golden whirlwind drives between them now.
Muse, with the rhythms of my thin voice, how

il ritmo della mia piccola voce?
Meglio fuggire dalla guerra atroce
del piacere, dell'oro, dell'alloro...

L'alloro... Oh! Bimbo semplice che fui,
200 dal cuore in mano e dalla fronte alta!
Oggi l'alloro è premio di colui
che tra clangor di buccine s'esalta,
che sale cerretano alla ribalta
per far di sé favoleggiar altrui...

205 «Avvocato, non parla: che cos'ha?»
«Oh! Signorina! Penso ai casi miei,
a piccole miserie, alla città...
Sarebbe dolce restar qui, con Lei!...» –
«Qui, nel solaio?...» – «Per l'eternità!» –
210 «Per sempre? Accetterebbe?...» – «Accetterei!»

Tacqui. Scorgevo un atropo soletto
e prigioniero. Stavasi in riposo
alla parete: il segno spaventoso
chiuso tra l'ali ripiegate a tetto.
215 Come lo vellicai sul corsaletto
si librò con un ronzo lamentoso.

«Che ronzo triste!» – «È la Marchesa in pianto...
La Dannata sarà che porta pena...»
Nulla s'udiva che la sfinge in pena
220 e dalle vigne, ad ora ad ora, un canto:
O mio carino tu mi piaci tanto,
siccome piace al mar una sirena...

Un richiamo s'alzò, querulo e rôco:
«È Maddalena inqueta che si tardi;
225 scendiamo; è l'ora della cena!» – «Guardi,

can I divert them from their crazy course?
Better to hide myself from the hideous wars
of pleasure, treasure, and the laurel bough . . .

The laurel . . . Lord, the simple child I was,
heart in my hand and head up in the air!
Today he plucks the laurel bough who does
his own promotion in the trumpet's blare,
the clown who climbs into the limelight where
he tells his fables and sells himself to us . . .

"Counselor, so quiet? Why don't you talk to me?"
"Signorina, I'm watching the fading view:
my life, the city, each petty misery . . .
How sweet it would be to stay here, with you . . ."
"Here, in the attic? . . ."—"For eternity!"
"Forever? Do you mean it? . . ."—"Yes, I do!"

Then I was silent. I noticed a death's-head
alone and imprisoned, hanging motionless
on the wall: its terrifying symbol was
hidden within its folded wings' pyramid.
I tickled it on the corselet, and as I did
it started to flutter with a plaintive buzz.

"What a sad moan!"—"It's the Marchesa's woe,
the doomed Marchesa bearing her agony . . ."
All we could hear was the sphinx's agony
and now and then a song from the fields below:
O my beloved one you please me so,
you please me as the sirens please the sea . . .

A call was rising, querulous and sore.
"It's Maddalena, she's cross because we're late.
Come, let's go down, it's time for dinner!"—"Wait,

guardi il tramonto, là... Com'è di fuoco!...
Restiamo ancora un poco!» – «Andiamo, è tardi!»
«Signorina, restiamo ancora un poco!...»

Le fronti al vetro, chini sulla piana,
230 seguimmo i neri pipistrelli, a frotte;
giunse col vento un ritmo di campana,
disparve il sole fra le nubi rotte;
a poco a poco s'annunciò la notte
sulla serenità canavesana...

235 «Una stella!...» - «Tre stelle!...» - «Quattro stelle!...»
«Cinque stelle!» - «Non sembra di sognare?...»
Ma ti levasti su quasi ribelle
alla perplessità crepuscolare:
«Scendiamo! È tardi: possono pensare
240 che noi si faccia cose poco belle...»

V

Ozi beati a mezzo la giornata,
nel parco dei Marchesi, ove la traccia
restava appena dell'età passata!
Le Stagioni camuse e senza braccia,
245 fra mucchi di letame e di vinaccia,
dominavano i porri e l'insalata.

L'insalata, i legumi produttivi
deridevano il busso delle aiole;
volavano le pieridi nel sole
250 e le cetonie e i bombi fuggitivi...
Io ti parlavo, piano, e tu cucivi
innebriata dalle mie parole.

look at that sunset . . . A flame! . . . Did you ever before—
Just a few minutes more!"—"Let's go, it's late!"
"Signorina, please, just a few minutes more! . . ."

Foreheads pressed to the glass, we leaned to see
the plain below. We followed the bats' flight.
Along the wind a bell tolled steadily,
along the sky the sun dropped out of sight
between the torn clouds. Bit by bit the night
covered the Canavesan serenity . . .

"A star!"—"Three stars!"—"No, four stars!"—"Five!"—
    "Don't you
feel that it's like a dream, feel yourself sinking?—"
But you jumped up, as if objecting to
the twilight's mystery, the shadows blinking:
"It's late! Let's go: or else they'll all start thinking
we're up here doing things we shouldn't do . . ."

V

Sweet idleness in the middle of the day,
in the park of the Marchesi, where there clung
hardly a trace of the ages fled away.
The armless Seasons with flattened noses, among
the dregs of pressed grapes and the piles of dung,
ruled over the leeks and lettuce in their sway.

The salad greens exuberantly growing
mocked the neat box of the flower bed.
The furtive bumblebees and beetles sped,
and in the sunlight butterflies were flowing . . .
Slowly I talked to you, and you sat sewing,
intoxicated with the words I said.

«Tutto mi spiace che mi piacque innanzi!
Ah! Rimanere qui, sempre, al suo fianco,
255 terminare la vita che m'avanzi
tra questo verde e questo lino bianco!
Se Lei sapesse come sono stanco
delle donne rifatte sui romanzi!

Vennero donne con proteso il cuore:
260 ognuna dileguò, senza vestigio.
Lei sola, forse, il freddo sognatore
educherebbe al tenero prodigio:
mai non comparve sul mio cielo grigio
quell'aurora che dicono: l'Amore...»

265 Tu mi fissavi... Nei begli occhi fissi
leggevo uno sgomento indefinito;
le mani ti cercai, sopra il cucito,
e te le strinsi lungamente, e dissi:
«Mia cara Signorina, se guarissi
270 ancora, mi vorrebbe per marito?»

«Perché mi fa tali discorsi vani?
Sposare, Lei, me brutta e poveretta!...»
E ti piegasti sulla tua panchetta
facendo al viso coppa delle mani,
275 simulando singhiozzi acuti e strani
per celia, come fa la scolaretta.

Ma, nel chinarmi su di te, m'accorsi
che sussultavi come chi singhiozza
veramente, né sa piú ricomporsi:
280 mi parve udire la tua voce mozza
da gli ultimi singulti nella strozza:
«Non mi ten...ga mai piú... tali dis...corsi!»

"All that once pleased me pleases me no more.
Ah, to stay here forever, at your side,
to end what's left of my life amid this pure
white linen and this bright green countryside.
If you knew how tired I am, how glassy-eyed
from all those women dressed in literature.

The women who offered me their hearts to hold,
without a trace they vanished one and all.
But you alone, perhaps, could lead the cold
dreamer to the tender miracle:
'Love': I wonder if it ever will
light up my gray sky with its streaks of gold . . ."

You stared . . . And in your fair eyes riveted
I read a half-afraid perplexity.
Over the sewing, I pulled your hands to me
and clutched them for a long time, and I said:
"My dearest Signorina, if I should
recover, would you want to marry me?"

"Why do you talk such nonsense? How could I,
so poor and ugly, ever marry you! . . ."
You huddled on your stool, your face withdrew
behind your cupped hands, and with wild and high
sobs you made believe you'd begun to cry,
the way that playful little schoolgirls do.

But then, as I leaned toward you, I began
to realize you were trembling like someone wracked
by real sobs, going all to pieces, and then
I thought I heard you say, in a voice attacked
by the last sobs in your throat, in a voice that cracked,
"Don't ever taaalk . . . that waaay to . . . meee a . . . gain!"

«Piange?» E tentai di sollevarti il viso
inutilmente. Poi, colto un fuscello,
285 ti vellicai l'orecchio, il collo snello...
Già tutta luminosa nel sorriso
ti sollevasti vinta d'improvviso,
trillando un trillo gaio di fringuello.

Donna: mistero senza fine bello!

VI

290 Tu m'hai amato. Nei begli occhi fermi
luceva una blandizie femminina;
tu civettavi con sottili schermi,
tu volevi piacermi, Signorina;
e piú d'ogni conquista cittadina
295 mi lusingò quel tuo voler piacermi!

Unire la mia sorte alla tua sorte
per sempre, nella casa centenaria!
Ah! Con te, forse, piccola consorte
vivace, trasparente come l'aria,
300 rinnegherei la fede letteraria
che fa la vita simile alla morte...

Oh! questa vita sterile, di sogno!
Meglio la vita ruvida concreta
del buon mercante inteso alla moneta,
305 meglio andare sferzati dal bisogno,
ma vivere di vita! Io mi vergogno,
sí, mi vergogno d'essere un poeta!

"You're crying?" And in vain I tried to raise
your face to mine. With a twig I stealthily
tickled your ear, your slim neck . . . Suddenly
you raised your head up, with a lustrous gaze
so full of smiles it set the day ablaze,
trilling a bright finch's trill for me.

Woman: an endless lovely mystery.

VI

You loved me. Those two steady eyes of yours
were shining with a feminine blandishment.
You flirted with me with your slender lures,
you wished to please me: Signorina, it meant
more than all city conquests to catch a hint
of the wish to please me in those eyes of yours.

To join my fate forever with your fate
in the hundred-year-old house up on the hill:
with you as my vivacious little mate,
transparent as the air, perhaps I'd kill
this literary faith that binds me still,
that grinds this life down to a deathlike state . . .

This life of dreams, this life of sterility:
better to find a rude rough row and hoe it,
to be a merchant after cash and show it,
better to be lashed by necessity,
but living, but alive! I'm ashamed to be—
yes, I confess, I'm ashamed to be a poet!

Tu non fai versi. Tagli le camicie
per tuo padre. Hai fatta la seconda
310 classe, t'han detto che la Terra è tonda,
ma tu non credi... E non mediti Nietzsche...
Mi piaci. Mi faresti piú felice
d'un'intellettuale gemebonda...

Tu ignori questo male che s'apprende
315 in noi. Tu vivi i tuoi giorni modesti,
tutta beata nelle tue faccende.
Mi piaci. Penso che leggendo questi
miei versi tuoi, non mi comprenderesti,
ed a me piace chi non mi comprende.

320 Ed io non voglio piú essere io!
Non piú l'esteta gelido, il sofista,
ma vivere nel tuo borgo natio,
ma vivere alla piccola conquista
mercanteggiando placido, in oblio
325 come tuo padre, come il farmacista...

Ed io non voglio piú essere io!

VII

Il farmacista nella farmacia
m'elogiava un farmaco sagace:
«Vedrà che dorme le sue notti in pace:
330 un sonnifero d'oro, in fede mia!»
Narrava, intanto, certa gelosia
con non so che loquacità mordace.

You don't make verse. You mend your father's britches.
You went to the local school for a year or two,
they told you that the World is round, but you
don't believe it . . . You don't read those books of
    Nietzsche's . . .
And more than all those intellectual leeches
you please me, and you'd make me happier too . . .

You're ignorant of this malignancy
that eats at us. You live your modest days
tending to household business happily.
You please me. If you read these lines in praise
of you, you wouldn't understand my ways,
and who misunderstands me pleases me.

And I don't want to be me anymore,
no more the cold aesthete, the casuist.
I want to live in the town where you were born,
I want to live for the little gain, unmissed,
obscurely farming or running a country store,
just like your father, just like the pharmacist . . .

And I don't want to be me anymore!

VII

The pharmacist inside his pharmacy
praised me a pharmaceutical miracle:
"You'll sleep just like a baby with this pill.
A golden soporific, believe you me!"
Meanwhile he told of a certain jealousy
with I don't know what flowing ridicule.

«Ma c'è il notaio pazzo di quell'oca!
Ah! quel notaio, creda: un capo ameno!
335 La Signorina è brutta, senza seno,
volgaruccia, Lei sa, come una cuoca...
E la dote... la dote è poca, poca:
diecimila, chi sa, forse nemmeno...»
«Ma dunque?» – «C'è il notaio furibondo
340 con Lei, con me che volli presentarla
a Lei; non mi saluta, non mi parla...» –
«È geloso?» – «Geloso! Un finimondo!...» –
«Pettegolezzi!...» – «Ma non Le nascondo
che temo, temo qualche brutta ciarla...» –
345 «Non tema! Parto.» – «Parte? E va lontana?» –
«Molto lontano... Vede, cade a mezzo
ogni motivo di pettegolezzo...» –
«Davvero parte? Quando?» – «In settimana...»
Ed uscii dall'odor d'ipecacuana
350 nel plenilunio settembrino, al rezzo.

Andai vagando nel silenzio amico,
triste perduto come un mendicante.
Mezzanotte scoccò, lenta, rombante
su quel dolce paese che non dico.
355 La Luna sopra il campanile antico
pareva «un punto sopra un I gigante».

In molti mesti e pochi sogni lieti,
solo pellegrinai col mio rimpianto
fra le siepi, le vigne, i castagneti
360 quasi d'argento fatti nell'incanto;
e al cancello sostai del camposanto
come s'usa nei libri dei poeti.

"But that goose has got the notary deranged!
That notary, who knows what's in his hat?
The Signorina's ugly, and she's flat,
and vulgar, like a cook . . . And what's more strange,
the dowry's next to nothing. It's small change,
maybe ten thousand, maybe less than that . . ."

"So?"—"So the notary's in a royal snit
at you, at me who introduced you two.
He doesn't talk to me, he snubs me too . . ."
"He's jealous?"—"Jealous! He's ready to throw a fit!"
"A lot of gossip!"—"There's no use hiding it,
I fear some ugly talk before we're through . . ."

"Don't fear! I'm leaving."—"Leaving? What do you know!
Going far?"—"Very far . . . So you needn't be afraid,
you'll see how fast this gossiping will fade . . ."
"So you're really leaving? When?"—"In a week or so . . ."
From the smell of ipecac I turned to go
through the full September moonlight, toward the shade.

In the friendly silence I began to roam,
as sad and lost as a beggar. And nearby
midnight struck slowly, rumbling through the sky
on that sweet countryside that I don't name.
The moon poised over the old steeple came
to seem like "a dot above a gigantic I."

In many sad and few happy reveries
I wandered on, alone with my regret,
past all the hedges, vineyards, chestnut trees
that glistened silver in the delicate
enchantment. At the cemetery gate
I paused, as one does in books of poetry.

Voi che posate già sull'altra riva,
immuni dalla gioia, dallo strazio,
365 parlate, o morti, al pellegrino sazio!
Giova guarire? Giova che si viva?
O meglio giova l'Ospite furtiva
che ci affranca dal Tempo e dallo Spazio?

A lungo meditai, senza ritrarre
370 le tempia dalle sbarre. Quasi a scherno
s'udiva il grido delle strigi alterno...
La Luna, prigioniera fra le sbarre,
imitava con sue luci bizzarre
gli amanti che si baciano in eterno.

375 Bacio lunare, fra le nubi chiare
come di moda settant'anni fa!
Ecco la Morte e la Felicità!
L'una m'incalza quando l'altra appare;
quella m'esilia in terra d'oltremare,
380 questa promette il bene che sarà...

VIII

Nel mestissimo giorno degli addii
mi piacque rivedere la tua villa.
La morte dell'estate era tranquilla
in quel mattino chiaro che salii
385 tra i vigneti già spogli, tra i pendii
già trapunti di bei colchici lilla.

Forse vedendo il bel fiore malvagio
che i fiori uccide e semina le brume,
le rondini addestravano le piume

You who already lie on the other shore,
immune from joy and from this grief of mine,
speak to a jaded pilgrim, give me a sign:
Should I recover? Should I live anymore?
Or should I bow to the creeping Visitor
who liberates us out of Space and Time?

I leaned my head against the bars in slow
sad meditation. Almost sneeringly
the hidden owls seemed to screech at me . . .
Imprisoned in the cold bars, in the glow
of its weird light the moon was a tableau
of lovers kissing through eternity.

And framed between the clouds, the kiss spoke clear
in the style of seventy years ago, to me:
Here look on Death and on Felicity!
One hounds me when the other one comes near:
one spurs me on to an alien hemisphere,
the other promises blessings yet to be . . .

VIII

On that most mournful day of our goodbyes,
seeing your villa brought me happiness.
Summer was dying in slow peacefulness
in the clear morning as I climbed the rise
past vineyards already barren, past hillsides
already embroidered with lilac crocuses.

Perhaps the sight of the beautiful malign
flower that kills the flowers and sows the haze
had warned the swallows it was time to raise

390 al primo volo, timido, randagio;
e a me randagio parve buon presagio
accompagnarmi loro nel costume.

«Vïaggio con le rondini stamane...» –
«Dove andrà?» – «Dove andrò? Non so... Vïaggio,
395 vïaggio per fuggire altro vïaggio...
Oltre Marocco, ad isolette strane,
ricche in essenze, in datteri, in banane,
perdute nell'Atlantico selvaggio...

Signorina, s'io torni d'oltremare,
400 non sarà d'altri già? Sono sicuro
di ritrovarla ancora? Questo puro
amore nostro salirà l'altare?»
E vidi la tua bocca sillabare
a poco a poco le sillabe: *giuro*.

405 Giurasti e disegnasti una ghirlanda
sul muro, di viole e di saette,
coi nomi e con la data memoranda:
trenta settembre novecentosette...
Io non sorrisi. L'animo godette
410 quel romantico gesto d'educanda.

Le rondini garrivano assordanti,
garrivano garrivano parole
d'addio, guizzando ratte come spole,
incitando le piccole migranti...
415 Tu seguivi gli stormi lontananti
ad uno ad uno per le vie del sole...

«Un altro stormo s'alza!...» – «Ecco s'avvia!» –
«Sono partite...» – «E non le salutò!...» –

their wings: and in this wandering mood of mine
I took their nervous fluttering for a sign
to follow them along their wandering ways.

"I'm leaving with the swallows . . ."—"Where will you go?"
"I don't know where I'm going . . . I have to journey,
I journey to escape another journey . . .
Beyond Morocco, where strange breezes blow,
where the banana plants and date palms grow
on islands lost in the wild Atlantic's churning . . .

And if the sea should bring me back again,
can I be sure I'll find you? Will you wear
another's ring? Or will the love we share,
this pure love, reach the altar rail?" And then
I watched you, watched your mouth as it began
slowly to form the syllables: *I swear*.

You swore, and drew a garland on the wall
of violets and arrows interwoven
with our two names, and underneath it all
September thirtieth Nineteen hundred seven . . .
I didn't smile. My spirit came alive in
the romantic gesture and the schoolgirl scrawl.

The swallows were twittering messages of goodbye,
twittering twittering deafeningly they spun
back and forth, whirling like shuttles, one by one
urging their young ones up into the sky . . .
You watched the flocks as they began to fly,
traveling down the highways of the sun . . .

"There goes another flock! . . ."—"Look, there they are!"
"They're gone . . ."—"And you didn't say goodbye to
    them! . . ."

«Lei devo salutare, quelle no:
420 quelle terranno la mia stessa via:
in un palmeto della Barberia
tra pochi giorni le ritroverò...»

Giunse il distacco, amaro senza fine,
e fu il distacco d'altri tempi, quando
425 le amate in bande lisce e in crinoline,
protese da un giardino venerando,
singhiozzavano forte, salutando
diligenze che andavano al confine...

M'apparisti cosí come in un cantico
430 del Prati, lacrimante l'abbandono
per l'isole perdute nell'Atlantico;
ed io fui l'uomo d'altri tempi, un buono
sentimentale giovine romantico...

Quello che fingo d'essere e non sono!

"It's you I have to bid goodbye, not them.
The birds and I are following the same star.
Two or three days from now, out in a far
Barbary palm grove, I'll see them again . . ."

Impossibly bitter, the moment of parting was here,
a moment out of another century, when,
leaning out of an ancient garden, dear
smooth-haired sweethearts clad in crinoline,
wracked with sobs, stretched out their arms in vain
toward diligences bound for the frontier . . .

You were a lady from Prati's lyrics, frantic,
abandoned in your sad perplexity
for the lost islands of the wild Atlantic.
And I was the man of another century,
a splendid sentimental young romantic . . .

The man I'm not, the man I pretend to be!

L'amica di nonna Speranza

> 28 giugno 1850
> «... alla sua Speranza
> la sua Carlotta...»
> (dall'album: dedica d'una fotografia)

I

Loreto impagliato ed il busto d'Alfieri, di Napoleone
i fiori in cornice (le buone cose di pessimo gusto),

il caminetto un po' tetro, le scatole senza confetti,
i frutti di marmo protetti dalle campane di vetro,

5 un qualche raro balocco, gli scrigni fatti di valve,
gli oggetti col monito *salve*, *ricordo*, le noci di cocco,

Venezia ritratta a musaici, gli acquarelli un po' scialbi,
le stampe, i cofani, gli albi dipinti d'anemoni arcaici,

le tele di Massimo d'Azeglio, le miniature,
10 i dagherottipi: figure sognanti in perplessità,

il gran lampadario vetusto che pende a mezzo il salone
e immilla nel quarzo le buone cose di pessimo gusto,

Grandmother Speranza's Friend

28 June 1850
" . . . to her Speranza
her Carlotta . . ."
(from the album: dedication of a photograph)

I

Poll parrot stuffed and the bust of Napoleon, of Alfieri,
the flowery moldings (the very good things in terrible taste),

the dark fireplace, the collection of boxes without any candy,
the clusters of marble fruit standing under the bell jars'
    protection,

the odd toy, the coconuts there, the box made of seashells,
    the warning
of *Pray* or *Remember* adorning the keepsakes that lie
    everywhere,

the albums with painted archaic wildflowers, an engraving or
    two,
the pale watercolors, the view of Venice done all in mosaic,

the miniatures there in profusion, a painting or two by
    d'Azeglio,
daguerrotypes (just a bit yellow) with figures in dreamy
    confusion,

the splendid old chandelier placed in the center, above the
    great hall:
a thousand reflections of all the good things in terrible taste,

il cúcu dell'ore che canta, le sedie parate a damasco
chèrmisi... rinasco, rinasco del mille ottocento cinquan-
   ta!

II

15 I fratellini alla sala quest'oggi non possono accedere
che cauti (hanno tolte le federe ai mobili. È giorno di
   gala).

Ma quelli v'irrompono in frotta. È giunta, è giunta in
   vacanza
la grande sorella Speranza con la compagna Carlotta!

Ha diciassett'anni la Nonna! Carlotta quasi lo stesso:
20 da poco hanno avuto il permesso d'aggiungere un cer-
   chio alla gonna,

il cerchio ampissimo increspa la gonna a rose turchine.
Piú snella da la crinoline emerge la vita di vespa.

Entrambe hanno uno scialle ad arance a fiori a uccelli a
   ghirlande;
divisi i capelli in due bande scendenti a mezzo le guancie.

25 Han fatto l'esame piú egregio di tutta la classe. Che af-
   fanno
passato terribile! Hanno lasciato per sempre il collegio.

the red damasked chairs, in the corner the cuckoo clock . . .
    All of them lift me
out of myself: I'm reborn in the year eighteen hundred and
    fifty!

II

The little boys have to beware when they come in the parlor
    today
(the dust covers, just for today, have been taken off all of the
    chairs).

But still they come galloping through. She's home on
    vacation (they've missed her),
Speranza is home, their big sister! Her comrade Carlotta's
    here too!

My Grandmother's seventeen now. Carlotta is almost as old:
and not long ago they were told that hoop skirts would now
    be allowed.

Now the widest of hoops ripples under a skirt lined with
    cobalt blue roses,
while crinoline tightly encloses a wasp-waist incredibly
    slender.

They've shawls decorated with little flowers oranges birds
    everywhere,
and they wear all the way to the middle of their cheeks the
    two bands of their hair.

Their exams were the finest of all in their class. What a
    terrible few
days they have just suffered through! Now they're finished
    forever with school.

Silenzio, bambini! Le amiche – bambini, fate pian piano! –
le amiche provano al piano un fascio di musiche antiche.

Motivi un poco artefatti nel secentismo fronzuto
30 di Arcangelo del Leúto e d'Alessandro Scarlatti.

Innamorati dispersi, gementi il *core* e l'*augello*,
languori del Giordanello in dolci bruttissimi versi:

> . . . .
> ... caro mio ben
> credimi almen!
35 senza di te
> languisce il cor!
> Il tuo fedel
> sospira ognor,
> cessa crudel
40 tanto rigor!
> . . . .

Carlotta canta. Speranza suona. Dolce e fiorita
si schiude alla breve romanza di mille promesse la vita.

O musica! Lieve sussurro! E già nell'animo ascoso
d'ognuna sorride lo sposo promesso: il Principe Azzurro,

Now children, be still if you please! The two—now be quiet,
    I say!—
the two friends are going to play some songs from the long-
    ago days.

Motifs just a little too arty, the leafy Baroque in full fruit,
by Arcangelo of the Lute and by Alessandro Scarlatti.

Parted lovers with spirits so mellow, wailing *heart* and *wing'd
    creature* and *swoon'd*,
sweet horrible versicles tuned to the languors of Giordanello:

....

. . . do but believe
for thee I grieve!
Heart longs for thee
on foreign shore!
For thee such sighs
forevermore,
who fill mine eyes
with weeping sore!

....

Carlotta sings, while Speranza plays piano. And in the brief
    song
flowering life opens its hands as its thousand bright promises
    throng.

In the music's susurrus they see, each one in her soul's secret
    place,
a smile just for her on the face of Prince Charming, her
    husband-to-be,

45 lo sposo dei sogni sognati... O margherite in collegio
sfogliate per sortilegio sui teneri versi del Prati!

III

Giungeva lo Zio, signore virtuoso, di molto riguardo,
ligio al passato, al Lombardo-Veneto, all'Imperatore;

giungeva la Zia, ben degna consorte, molto dabbene,
50 ligia al passato, sebbene amante del Re di Sardegna...

«Baciate la mano alli Zii!» – dicevano il Babbo e la
 Mamma,
e alzavano il volto di fiamma ai piccolini restii.

«E questa è l'amica in vacanza: madamigella Carlotta
Capenna: l'alunna piú dotta, l'amica piú cara a Speranza».

55 «Ma bene... ma bene... ma bene...» – diceva gesuitico e
 tardo
lo Zio di molto riguardo – «... ma bene... ma bene... ma
 bene...

Capenna? Conobbi un Arturo Capenna... Capenna...
 Capenna...
Sicuro! Alla Corte di Vienna! Sicuro... sicuro... sicuro...»

the husband who's kissed her already, in dreams . . . In the
   long days at school
all the petals of daisies they pulled to the tenderest verses of
   Prati!

III

Came the Uncle, whom all knew to be a man of most
   virtuous temper,
loyal to the past, to the Emperor, and to royal Lombardy-
   Venetia.

Came the Aunt, his fit mate, of opinions most worthy, and
   upright of mind,
loyal to the past, though inclined to admire the King of
   Sardinia . . .

"Kiss your dear Aunt and Uncle!" was what both the
   Mamma and Papa then said,
bearing down with bright faces of red on the children who'd
   much rather not.

"And may we present Mademoiselle Carlotta Capenna, a girl
who's an excellent scholar, as well as Speranza's best friend in
   the world."

"Very nice . . . very nice . . . very nice . . ."—jesuitically,
   ever so slowly
came the words of the Uncle so wholly esteemed—"very nice
   . . . very nice . . .

Capenna? I knew an Arturo Capenna . . . Capenna . . .
   Capenna . . .
To be sure! At the Court of Vienna! To be sure . . . to be
   sure . . . to be sure . . ."

«Gradiscono un po' di moscato?» «Signora Sorella magari...»
60 E con un sorriso pacato sedevano in bei conversari.

«... ma la Brambilla non seppe...» – È pingue già per l'*Ernani*...
«La Scala non ha piú soprani...» – «Che vena quel Verdi... Giuseppe

«... nel Marzo avremo un lavoro alla Fenice, m'han detto,
nuovissimo: il *Rigoletto*. Si parla d'un capolavoro».

65 «... Azzurri si portano o grigi?» – «E questi orecchini? Che bei
rubini! E questi cammei...» – «la gran novità di Parigi...»

«... Radetzky? Ma che? L'armistizio... la pace, la pace che regna...
«... quel giovine Re di Sardegna è uomo di molto giudizio!»

«È certo uno spirito insonne, e forte e vigile e scaltro...»
70 «È bello?» – «Non bello: tutt'altro». – «Gli piacciono molto le donne...»

«Speranza!» (chinavansi piano, in tono un po' sibillino) «Carlotta! Scendete in giardino: andate a giocare al volano!»

Allora le amiche serene lasciavano con un perfetto inchino di molto rispetto gli Zii molto dabbene.

"Would you care for some muscatel?"—"That would be a most welcome libation."
And so with a calm smile they sat themselves down for some good conversation.

". . . Brambilla? No voice . . ."—"And what hips! She's already too fat for *Ernani* . . ."
"La Scala has no more soprani . . ."—"This Verdi's on everyone's lips . . ."

". . . in March we're to have a new piece at the Phoenix, so everyone's said.
Rigoletto: brand new, never played. And already they say 'masterpiece'."

". . . What are they wearing this year, blue or gray?"—"And those earrings? And those
lovely rubies! And those cameos! . . ."—"All the latest from Paris, my dear . . ."

" . . . Radetzky? Eh? Peace, it appears . . . the armistice . . ."—"In my opinion,
as young as he is, that Sardinian King has the wisdom of years!"

"And a spirit that doesn't know fear, shrewd and tireless, ever alert . . ."
"And handsome?"—"No, quite the reverse."—"Quite an eye for the ladies, I hear . . ."

"Speranza!" (the call softly came, in a tone just a bit sibylline)
"Carlotta! The weather's so fine: on the lawn there's a shuttlecock game!"

Serenely the young ladies went, after curtseying delicately, with respect in the highest degree, to the most worthy Uncle and Aunt.

IV

75 Oimè! che giocando un volano, troppo respinto all'assalto,
non piú ridiscese dall'alto dei rami d'un ippocastano!

S'inchinano sui balaustri le amiche e guardano il lago
sognando l'amore presago nei loro bei sogni trilustri.

«Ah! se tu vedessi che bei denti!» – «Quant'anni?...»
– «Ventotto».
80 «Poeta?» – «Frequenta il salotto della contessa Maffei!»

Non vuole morire, non langue il giorno. S'accende piú
  ancora
di porpora: come un'aurora stigmatizzata di sangue;

si spenge infine, ma lento. I monti s'abbrunano in coro:
il Sole si sveste dell'oro, la Luna si veste d'argento.

85 Romantica Luna fra un nimbo leggiero, che baci le chiome
dei pioppi, arcata siccome un sopracciglio di bimbo,

il sogno di tutto un passato nella tua curva s'accampa:
non sorta sei da una stampa del *Novelliere Illustrato*?

IV

Alas! As they play merrily, one swings too hard on the return,
and the shuttlecock never returns from the limbs of a horse-chestnut tree.

They gaze where the lake water gleams, they lean where the balustrades hold them,
they dream of the great love foretold them in lovely fifteen-year-old's dreams.

"How old?"—"Twenty-eight. And each one of those beautiful teeth shines like sequins!"
"And is he a poet?"—"He frequents the Countess Maffei's *salon*!"

Unwilling to die, the day lingers. The sky turns rich purple: the heightening
resembles a dawn almost frightening, arriving with long bloody fingers.

But slowly, at last, day is gone. The mountains grow dark with the sky:
the Sun puts his golden coat by, the Moon puts her silver dress on.

Romantic young Moon in a mild nimbus, who kisses with silver
the leaves of the poplars, a sliver arched like the brows of a child,

your curve holds a past that's created in dreams: aren't you just a kind
of engraving one's likely to find in the pages of *Tales Illustrated*?

Vedesti le case deserte di Parisina la bella?
90 Non forse non forse sei quella amata dal giovine Werther?

«... mah! Sogni di là da venire!» – «Il Lago s'è fatto
   piú denso
di stelle» – «... che pensi?» – «... Non penso.» – «... Ti
   piacerebbe morire?»

«Sí! – «Pare che il cielo riveli piú stelle nell'acqua e
   piú lustri.
Inchínati sui balaustri: sognamo cosí, tra due cieli...»

95 «Son come sospesa! Mi libro nell'alto...» – «Conosce
   Mazzini...»
– «E l'ami?...» – «Che versi divini!» – «Fu lui a donarmi quel libro,

ricordi? che narra siccome, amando senza fortuna,
un tale si uccida per una, per una che aveva il mio nome».

V

Carlotta! nome non fine, ma dolce che come l'essenze
100 resusciti le diligenze, lo scialle, la crinoline...

Amica di Nonna, conosco le aiole per ove leggesti
i casi di Jacopo mesti nel tenero libro del Foscolo.

Did you see the dark house where the murder of fair Parisina
   was done?
And you, perhaps you are the one so loved by the luckless
   young Werther?

". . . who knows! Dreams and hopes!"—"How the sky drops
   more stars in the Lake all the time."
". . . What are you thinking of?"—". . . I'm not thinking."—
". . . Would you like to die?"

"Oh yes!"—"Now look how it lies all aglitter with stars
   everywhere.
Lean over the balustrade: there, we're dreaming between the
   two skies . . ."

"I'm suspended, I'm hovering! Look . . ."—"He knows
   Mazzini, you know . . ."
"And you love him?"—"What verses, they're so divine!"—
"And remember that book

I was reading? He gave it to me. That book with the unhappy
   lover,
the fellow who kills himself over the girl with the same name
   as me."

V

Carlotta! Your name's not a song, but like a rare perfume it
   calls
up a world of young women in shawls and diligences
   creaking along . . .

Friend of Grandmother Speranza, I walk past the flower beds
   where
you read of young Ortis' despair in Foscolo's tender romance.

Ti fisso nell'albo con tanza tristezza, ov'è di tuo pugno
la data: *ventotto di giugno del mille ottocentocinquanta.*

105 Stai come rapita in un cantico: lo sguardo al cielo profondo
e l'indice al labbro, secondo l'atteggiamento romantico.

Quel giorno – malinconia – vestivi un abito rosa,
per farti – novissima cosa! – ritrarre in *fotografia*...

Ma te non rivedo nel fiore, amica di Nonna! Ove sei
110 o sola che, forse, potrei amare, amare d'amore?

Here you are in the album: it gives me such sadness to look at the date
written there in your hand: *twenty-eighth of June eighteen hundred and fifty.*

As if rapt in a lyric, impassioned, you gaze heavenward, with one small
finger beside your lips, all in the height of a long-ago fashion.

That day—melancholy reflections possess me now—you were arrayed
all in pink for the portrait they made with the *camera*—the latest invention.

But I can't find you now in your prime, Grandmother's friend! Where've you gone,
you who might be the woman, the one I could love, I could love for all time?

Cocotte

I

Ho rivisto il giardino, il giardinetto
contiguo, le palme del viale,
la cancellata rozza dalla quale
mi protese la mano ed il confetto...

II

5 «Piccolino, che fai solo soletto?»
«Sto giocando al Diluvio Universale».
Accennai gli stromenti, le bizzarre
cose che modellavo nella sabbia,
ed ella si chinò come chi abbia
10 fretta d'un bacio e fretta di ritrarre
la bocca, e mi baciò di tra le sbarre
come si bacia un uccellino in gabbia.

Sempre ch'io viva rivedrò l'incanto
di quel suo volto tra le sbarre quadre!
15 La nuca mi serrò con mani ladre;
ed io stupivo di vedermi accanto
al viso, quella bocca tanto, tanto
diversa dalla bocca di mia Madre!

«Piccolino, ti piaccio che mi guardi?
20 Sei qui pei bagni? Ed affittate là?»
«Sí... vedi la mia Mamma e il mio Papà?»
Subito mi lasciò, con negli sguardi
un vano sogno (ricordai piú tardi)
un vano sogno di maternità...

Cocotte

I

I've seen the little garden once again,
the one next door to it, the palm trees trailing
leaves down the avenue, the rusted railing
where the hand appeared with a piece of candy then . . .

II

"What are you doing there, my little man,
so all alone?"—"Making Noah's Ark go sailing."

I showed her my pail and shovel, and my array,
molded from sand, of odd-shaped statuary,
and she bent down like someone in a hurry
to give a kiss and quickly pull away
and kissed me through the railing, just the way
you'd stoop to peck a kiss at a caged canary.

As long as I live I'll see it perfectly,
the enchantment of her face between the bars.
She took me in those thieving hands of hers,
by the nape: and I sat there amazed to see
that face bend down, that mouth come close to me—
so different from my mother's mouth it was!

"Do you like to look at me? Do you think I'm nice?
Here for the baths? Is that big house for you?"
"Yes . . . Look, there's Mamma, see? There's Papa too!"
Then suddenly she left me, in her eyes
a dream (much later I would realize)
of motherhood that never could come true . . .

25 «Una cocotte!...»
            «Che vuol dire, mammina?»
«Vuol dire una cattiva signorina:
non bisogna parlare alla vicina!»
Co-co-tte... La strana voce parigina
dava alla mia fantasia bambina
30 un senso buffo d'ovo e di gallina...

Pensavo deità favoleggiate:
i naviganti e l'Isole Felici...
Co-co-tte... le fate intese a malefici
con cibi e con bevande affatturate...
35 Fate saranno, chi sa quali fate,
e in chi sa quali tenebrosi offici!

III

Un giorno – giorni dopo – mi chiamò
tra le sbarre fiorite di verbene:
«O piccolino, non mi vuoi piú bene!...»
40 «È vero che tu sei una cocotte?»
Perdutamente rise... E mi baciò
con le pupille di tristezza piene.

IV

Tra le gioie defunte e i disinganni,
dopo vent'anni, oggi si ravviva
45 il tuo sorriso... Dove sei, cattiva
Signorina? Sei viva? Come inganni
(meglio per te non essere piú viva!)
la discesa terribile degli anni?

"A cocotte! . . ."
        "Mamma, what does that word mean?"
"It means a wicked lady who lives in sin:
I don't want you to talk to her again!"
Co-co-tte . . . A word, a strange Parisian one,
that conjured in my infant fancies then
a comic image of an egg and hen . . .

I thought of mariners wandering on the oceans,
the fabled deities and the Happy Isles . . .
Co-co-tte . . . evil fairies at their wiles,
poisoning food and drink with magic potions . . .
Fairies they were, with who knows what dark notions,
and smiling who knows what dark fairy smiles!

III

One day—a few days later—she called me, through
the bars with bright verbena overrun:
"Don't you love me anymore, my little man? . . ."
"Mamma says you're a cocotte: is it true?"
She laughed then, desperately . . . As her eyes grew
filled up with sadness, she kissed me once again.

IV

Amid dead joys and disillusionments,
twenty years later your smile is bright once more . . .
My wicked lady, I wonder where you are.
Are you still living? And with what pretense
(much better if you're not living anymore!)
do you hide the years and all their dread descents?

Oimè! Da che non giova il tuo belletto
50 e il cosmetico già fa mala prova
l'ultimo amante disertò l'alcova...
Uno, sol uno: il piccolo folletto
che donasti d'un bacio e d'un confetto,
dopo vent'anni, oggi, ti ritrova

55 in sogno, e t'ama, in sogno, e dice: T'amo!
Da quel mattino dell'infanzia pura
forse ho amato te sola, o creatura!
Forse ho amato te sola! E ti richiamo!
Se leggi questi versi di richiamo
60 ritorna a chi t'aspetta, o creatura!

Vieni. Che importa se non sei più quella
che mi baciò quattrenne? Oggi t'agogno,
o vestita di tempo! Oggi ho bisogno
del tuo passato! Ti rifarò bella
65 come Carlotta, come Graziella,
come tutte le donne del mio sogno!

Il mio sogno è nutrito d'abbandono,
di rimpianto. Non amo che le rose
che non colsi. Non amo che le cose
70 che potevano essere e non sono
state... Vedo la casa, ecco le rose
del bel giardino di vent'anni or sono!

Oltre le sbarre il tuo giardino intatto
fra gli eucalipti liguri si spazia...
75 Vieni! T'accoglierà l'anima sazia.
Fa ch'io riveda il tuo volto disfatto;
ti bacierò; rifiorirà, nell'atto,
sulla tua bocca l'ultima tua grazia.

Alas, what use is the make-up you'd put on,
now it can no more make you look so gay,
now that the last lover has turned away . . .
One, only one (you called him your little man,
you gave him kisses and a candy then),
twenty years later, finds you again today

in a dream, and loves you, in a dream, and calls
"I love you!" From that pure morning so long gone
perhaps I've loved you only, little one.
Perhaps I've loved you only   And I recall.
And if you read these verses of recall
return to the one who awaits you, little one.

Though you're no longer the one who kissed me then
I desire you, I want to make you mine.
I need your past, my woman dressed in time.
Come. I will make you beautiful again
like Graziella, like Carlotta, and
like all the women of this dream of mine.

Abandonment and fond regret are still
the nurturers of my dream. I love only that
rose that I never plucked. I love only what
could once have come to be and never will . . .
The house, the roses in the garden plot
of twenty years ago, I see them still.

Behind the bars your garden spreads, intact
beneath the Ligurian eucalyptus tree . . .
This sated soul will greet you tenderly.
Let me see once more your face that time has cracked.
I'll kiss you, kiss you deeply. In the act
your final grace will blossom forth for me.

Vieni! Sarà come se a me, per mano,
80 tu riportassi me stesso d'allora.
Il bimbo parlerà con la Signora.
Risorgeremo dal tempo lontano.
Vieni! Sarà come se a te, per mano,
io riportassi te, giovine ancora.

Come! It will be as if you took my hand
and brought me to the child that I was then.
The boy will talk to the Lady once again.
We'll rise together from time's distant land.
Come! It will be as if I took your hand
and brought you to your self, young once again.

III

The Veteran

☆

Il reduce

Totò Merúmeni

I

Col suo giardino incolto, le sale vaste, i bei
balconi secentisti guarniti di verzura,
la villa sembra tolta da certi versi miei,
sembra la villa-tipo, del Libro di Lettura...

5 Pensa migliori giorni la villa triste, pensa
gaie brigate sotto gli alberi centenari,
banchetti illustri nella sala da pranzo immensa
e danze nel salone spoglio da gli antiquari.

Ma dove in altri tempi giungeva Casa Ansaldo,
10 Casa Rattazzi, Casa d'Azeglio, Casa Oddone,
s'arresta un'automobile fremendo e sobbalzando,
villosi forestieri picchiano la gorgòne.

S'ode un latrato e un passo, si schiude cautamente
la porta... In quel silenzio di chiostro e di caserma
15 vive Totò Merúmeni con una madre inferma,
una prozia canuta ed uno zio demente.

II

Totò ha venticinque anni, tempra sdegnosa,
molta cultura e gusto in opere d'inchiostro,
scarso cervello, scarsa morale, spaventosa
20 chiaroveggenza: è il vero figlio del tempo nostro.

Totò Merúmeni

I

With its garden growing wild, with its seventeenth-century
balconies decked with green, with its huge rooms, it looks
like a villa taken from some piece of my poetry,
like a typical villa from the children's Lesson-Books . . .

Now the villa is sad, hoarding happier memories
of famous feasts they held in the cavernous dining halls,
bright parties underneath the hundred-year-old trees,
dances in the salon the dealers have stripped to the walls.

Here where in other times all the reigning families
came to call—Ansaldo, Rattazzi, d'Azeglio, Oddone, and
    more—
an auto shakes and sputters and stops under the trees,
shaggy foreigners pound the Gorgon's-head on the door.

A dog barks, a foot falls, and slowly the door will creak
open . . . In this silence of barracks, of monkish cell,
Totò Merúmeni lives with a mother who isn't well,
a great aunt white with age, and an uncle whose brains are
    weak.

II

Totò is twenty-five, has an attitude of disdain,
culture up to his ears, good taste in books and rhymes,
frightening clairvoyance, scant morals, scanty brain:
the true child, in a word, of these our modern times.

Non ricco, giunta l'ora di «vender parolette»
(il suo Petrarca!...) e farsi baratto o gazzettiere,
Totò scelse l'esilio. E in libertà riflette
ai suoi trascorsi che sarà bello tacere.

25 Non è cattivo. Manda soccorso di danaro
al povero, all'amico un cesto di primizie;
non è cattivo. A lui ricorre lo scolaro
pel tema, l'emigrante per le commendatizie.

Gelido, consapevole di sé e dei suoi torti,
30 non è cattivo. È il *buono* che derideva il Nietzsche
«... in verità derido l'inetto che si dice
buono, perché non ha l'ugne abbastanza forti...»

Dopo lo studio grave, scende in giardino, gioca
coi suoi dolci compagni sull'erba che l'invita;
35 i suoi compagni sono: una ghiandaia rôca,
un micio, una bertuccia che ha nome Makakita...

III

La Vita si ritolse tutte le sue promesse.
Egli sognò per anni l'Amore che non venne,
sognò pel suo martirio attrici e principesse
40 ed oggi ha per amante la cuoca diciottenne.

He isn't a wealthy man: the day came for him to be
a "word-vendor" (his Petrarch!), turn swindler or scribbler.
    Instead
Totò selected exile. He reflects in his liberty
on those weaknesses of his that are better left unsaid.

He's not really bad at heart. He sends money to help the
        poor,
of the garden's first fruits he makes up baskets for his friends:
he's not really bad at heart. The schoolboy comes to his door
for an essay, the emigrant comes for a letter of reference.

Cold-natured, and aware of himself and all his faults,
he's not really bad at heart. He's the *good man*, that fool of
        Nietzsche's:
". . . I've nothing but contempt for that imbecile they teach
        us
is good, when his claws are dull: too weak for anything
        else . . ."

After deep study, he goes down to the garden to play
with his sweet companions where the welcoming grasses
        grow.
And these companions of his are three: a screeching jay,
a tom-cat, a Barbary ape whose name is Little Magot . . .

III

One by one Life took all of its promises back.
For years and years he dreamed of Love he's never seen,
actresses and princesses he dreamed of, on the rack,
and now his mistress is the cook, who's just eighteen.

Quando la casa dorme, la giovinetta scalza,
fresca come una prugna al gelo mattutino,
giunge nella sua stanza, lo bacia in bocca, balza
su lui che la possiede, beato e resupino...

IV

45 Totò non può sentire. Un lento male indomo
inaridí le fonti prime del sentimento;
l'analisi e il sofisma fecero di quest'uomo
ciò che le fiamme fanno d'un edificio al vento.

Ma come le ruine che già seppero il fuoco
50 esprimono i giaggioli dai bei vividi fiori,
quell'anima riarsa esprime a poco a poco
una fiorita d'esili versi consolatori...

V

Cosí Totò Merúmeni, dopo tristi vicende,
quasi è felice. Alterna l'indagine e la rima.
55 Chiuso in se stesso, medita, s'accresce, esplora, intende
la vita dello Spirito che non intese prima.

Perché la voce è poca, e l'arte prediletta
immensa, perché il Tempo – mentre ch'io parlo! – va,
Totò opra in disparte, sorride, e meglio aspetta.
60 E vive. Un giorno è nato. Un giorno morirà.

When the house is all asleep, the barefoot girl slips out,
fresh as a little plum in the chilly morning air,
comes quietly to his room, kisses him on the mouth,
leaps on him: he enjoys her as he blissfully lies there . . .

IV

Totò can't feel a thing. An incurable slow evil
dried the early freshets of feeling all away.
Analysis and sophistry did to this poor devil
what flames do to a building on a windy day.

But just as in the rubble after a fire surges
a spray of gladioli blooms unexpectedly,
so it is with his parched soul: bit by bit emerges
a slender spray of verses, consoling poetry . . .

V

Thus Totò Merúmeni, after such a sad career,
is almost happy. He moves between inquiry and rhyme.
Closed with himself, he thinks, explores, expands, sees clear
the life of the Spirit that seemed so cloudy at one time.

Because the voice is small, and the treasured art is vast,
because—even as I tell you!—Time goes rushing by,
Totò smiles, works apart, waits for better things at last.
So he lives on. One day he was born. One day he'll die.

Una risorta

I

«Chiesi di voi: nessuno
sa l'eremo profondo
di questo morto al mondo.
Son giunta! V'importuno?»
5 «No!... Sono un po' smarrito
per vanità: non oso
dirvi: Son vergognoso
del mio rude vestito.

Trovate il buon compagno
10 molto mutato, molto
rozzo, barbuto, incolto,
in giubba di fustagno!...»

«Oh! Guido! Tra di noi!
Pel mio dolce passato,
15 in giubba o in isparato
Voi siete sempre Voi...»

Muta, come chi pensa
casi remoti e vani,
mi strinse le due mani
20 con tenerezza immensa.

E in quella famigliare
mitezza di sorella
forse intravidi quella
che avrei potuto amare.

A Woman Resurrected

I

"I asked for you: none knew
the deep sequestered world
of this man dead to the world.
I'm here! I'm disturbing you?"

"No, not at all! . . . It's just
my vanity . . . I'm afraid
to tell you: I'm dismayed
at the way you find me dressed.

That good companion of yours
is altered now, transformed:
unkempt, unshaved, unshorn,
in a rumpled suit of clothes . . ."

"Oh, Guido, between us two,
who shared so sweet a past!
In a sweater or in a vest
You always will be You . . ."

Then silently she pressed
my hands (she seemed like one
recalling something gone)
with infinite tenderness.

Her sisterly fingers moved
with intimate softness. Perhaps
I caught a distant glimpse
of the woman I could have loved.

II

25 «È come un sonno blando,
un ben senza tripudio;
leggo lavoro studio
ozio filosofando...

La mia vita è soave
30 oggi, senza perché;
levata s'è da me
non so qual cosa grave...»

«Il Desiderio! Amico,
il Desiderio ucciso
35 vi dà questo sorriso
calmo di saggio antico...

Ah! Voi beato! Io
nel mio sogno errabondo
soffro di tutto il mondo
40 vasto che non è mio!

Ancor sogno un'aurora
che gli occhi miei non videro;
desidero, desidero
terribilmente ancora!...»

45 Guardava i libri, i fiori,
la mia stanza modesta:
«È la tua stanza questa?
Dov'è che tu lavori?»

«Là, nel laboratorio
50 delle mie poche fedi...»
Passammo tra gli arredi
di quel mondo illusorio.

II

"Like a mild sleep it lies,
no exulting now, all steady.
I read, I work, I study,
I loaf, I philosophize . . .

My life flows easily
these days, meandering . . .
I don't know what heavy thing
has been lifted up from me . . ."

"Desire! It's slain desire
that has given you the calm
smile that you wear, like some
ancient philosopher . . .

How blest you are! I pine
in my wandering dream for the vast
world that I can't hold fast,
for the world that isn't mine!

On and on I dream a dawn
my eyes have yet to see.
I desire so terribly,
I desire on and on! . . ."

Her looks went everywhere:
books, plants, the simple room.
"And so this is your room.
Where do you work?"—"Out there,

in the laboratory. There blossom
my few beliefs . . ." We strayed
past the furnishings that made
that illusive microcosm.

Fruscì nella cornice
severa la sottana,
55 passò quella mondana
grazia profanatrice...

«E questi sali gialli
in questo vetro nero?»
«Medito un gran mistero:
60 l'amore dei cristalli».

«Amano?!...» – «A certi segni
pare. Già i saggi chini
cancellano i confini,
uniscono i Tre Regni.

65 Nel disco della lente
s'apre l'ignoto abisso,
già sotto l'occhio fisso
la pietra vive, sente...

Cadono i dogmi e l'uso
70 della Materia. In tutto
regna l'Essenza, in tutto
lo Spirito è diffuso...»

Mi stava ad ascoltare
con le due mani al mento
75 maschio, lo sguardo intento
tra il vasto arco cigliare,

cosí svelta di forme
nella guaina rosa,
la nera chioma ondosa
80 chiusa nel casco enorme.

There in the narrow space
her skirt began to rustle,
profaning with a bustle
of fashionable grace . . .

"And those black bottles of
yellow salts?"—"Ah, you see
I muse a great mystery:
the love of crystals."—"They love?"

"They seem to. There are signs.
There are brilliant pioneers
erasing the frontiers,
uniting the three reigns.

Those depths so long unknown
are pierced under the lens.
Intent, the eye can sense
the breathing of a stone . . .

The customs and the creeds
of Matter fall. In all
The Essence reigns, in all
the living Spirit breathes . . ."

She listened quietly,
her hands held at the sides
of her firm chin, her eyes
fixed earnestly on me

under her lashes' sweep,
her hair formed in a thick
black helmet, a sheath of pink
round her so slender shape.

«Ed in quell'urna appesa
con quella fitta rete?»
«Dormono cento quete
crisalidi in attesa...»

85 «Fammi vedere... Oh! Strane!
Son d'oro come bei
pendenti... Ed io vorrei
foggiarmene collane!

Gemme di stile egizio
90 sembrano...» – «O gnomi od anche
mute regine stanche
sopite in malefizio...»

«Le segui per vedere
lor fasi e lor costume?»
95 «Sí, medito un volume
su queste prigioniere.

Le seguo d'ora in ora
con pazienza estrema;
dirò su questo tema
100 cose non dette ancora».

Chini su quelle vite
misteriose e belle,
ragionavamo delle
crisalidi sopite.

105 Ma come una sua ciocca
mi vellicò sul viso,
mi volsi d'improvviso
e le baciai la bocca.

"And hanging in the net
in this basket, what are these?"
"A hundred chrysalides.
They sleep quietly and wait . . ."

"Let me see . . . Oh! They're gold,
like little charms! . . . I'd love
to fashion a necklace of
these pendants, so like old

Egyptian gems."—"They seem
like gnomes, or else a swarm
of tired queens becalmed
in a mad enchanter's dream . . ."

"You watch them to observe
their customs and their stages?"
"Yes, I'm musing many pages
on these little prisoners.

I watch them hour by hour,
I sit day after day.
And on this theme I'll say
things never said before."

And leaning over these
lovely mysterious creatures,
we talked about the natures
of becalmed chrysalides.

A lock of her hair broke free
and brushed my face, and then
I turned her face to mine
and kissed her suddenly.

  Sentii l'urtare sordo
110 del cuore, e nei capelli
  le gemme degli anelli,
  l'ebbrezza del ricordo...

  Vidi le nari fini,
  riseppi le sagaci
115 labbra e commista ai baci
  l'asprezza dei canini,

  e quel s'abbandonare,
  quel sogguardare blando,
  simile a chi sognando
120 desidera sognare...

I sensed the muffled beat
of the pounding heart, the shine
of earrings, the heady wine
of a rush of memories . . .

I saw the delicate
nostrils, I knew again
the expert lips, and then
the little teeth that bit,

and that mad abandoning,
that mild look once again,
just like a dreaming man
who wishes it were a dream . . .

Un'altra risorta

Solo, errando cosí come chi erra
senza meta, un po' triste, a passi stanchi,
udivo un passo frettoloso ai fianchi;
poi l'ombra apparve, e la conobbi in terra...
5 Tremante a guisa d'uom ch'aspetta guerra,
mi volsi e vidi i suoi capelli: bianchi.

Ma fu l'incontro mesto, e non amaro.
Proseguimmo tra l'oro delle acace
del Valentino, camminando a paro.
10 Ella parlava, tenera, loquace,
del passato, di sé, della sua pace,
del futuro, di me, del giorno chiaro.

«Che bel Novembre! È come una menzogna
primaverile! E lei, compagno inerte,
15 se ne va solo per le vie deserte,
col trasognato viso di chi sogna...
Fare bisogna. Vivere bisogna
la bella vita dalle mille offerte».

«Le mille offerte... Oh! vana fantasia!
20 Solo in disparte dalla molta gente,
ritrovo i sogni e le mie fedi spente,
solo in disparte l'anima s'oblía...
Vivo in campagna, con una prozia,
la madre inferma ed uno zio demente.

Another Resurrected

Alone, and wandering like a wanderer
without an aim, a little sad, with tired
steps, I heard hurried footsteps at my side,
then saw the shadow: recognizing her,
shuddering like a man expecting war,
I turned and looked at her: her hair was white.

But it was a sad encounter, it wasn't bitter.
We moved along among the gold acacias
of the Valentino park, walking together.
And she was talking, tender and loquacious,
about the past, herself, her self-possession,
about the future, me, and the bright weather.

"What a beautiful November! It's like a lie
of spring! And you, my limp companion, who goes
alone through all the empty avenues
with the dreamy face of a dreamer, sighing a sigh,
you've got to learn to live. You've got to try
this lovely life with its thousand promises."

"Promises . . . Empty disillusionment!
Alone, apart, far from the madding crowd
I find my dreams again and the faith I had,
alone, apart, forgetting: that's what I want . . .
I live in the countryside with a great aunt,
an invalid mother, an uncle weak in the head.

25 Sono felice. La mia vita è tanto
pari al mio sogno: il sogno che non varia:
vivere in una villa solitaria,
senza passato piú, senza rimpianto:
appartenersi, meditare... Canto
30 l'esilio e la rinuncia volontaria».

«Ah! lasci la rinuncia che non dico,
lasci l'esilio a me, lasci l'oblío
a me che rassegnata già m'avvio
prigioniera del Tempo, del nemico...
35 Dove Lei sale c'è la luce, amico!
Dov'io scendo c'è l'ombra, amico mio!...

Ed era lei che mi parlava, quella
che risorgeva dal passato eterno
sulle tepide soglie dell'inverno?...
40 La quarantina la faceva bella,
diversamente bella: una sorella
buona, dall'occhio tenero materno.

Tacevo, preso dalla grazia immensa
di quel profilo forte che m'adesca;
45 tra il cupo argento della chioma densa
ella appariva giovenile e fresca
come una deità settecentesca...
«Amico neghittoso, a che mai pensa?»

«Penso al Petrarca che raggiunto fu
50 per via, da Laura, com'io son da Lei...»
Sorrise, rise discoprendo i bei
denti... «Che Laura in fior di gioventú!...
Irriverente!... Pensi invece ai miei
capelli grigi... Non mi tingo piú».

I'm happy there. My life's a perfect fit
with my dream, a dream without a deviation:
my villa in its splendid isolation,
a life without a past, without regret,
doing what suits me, musing . . . I celebrate
exile and free-willed renunciation."

"Leave that renunciation here with me,
leave me the exile and oblivion.
I am resigned. Already I've become
the prisoner of Time, the enemy . . .
Where you rise up, the light is shining free,
where I go down, the shadows start to form . . ."

And was it she who talked so, was it she
arisen out of an everlasting past
to stand at winter's wan threshold at last? . . .
Her forty years had made her seem to me
beautiful in a new way: sisterly,
with eyes of a tender and maternal cast.

Now I was silent, taken by the intense
grace of her strong profile. Alluringly
framed in the dark silver of her dense
hair, she seemed fresh and youthful, she seemed to me
like a goddess of the eighteenth century.
"What goes on in your head, my listless friend?"

"I was thinking of Petrarch, overtaken by Laura
the way I was by you, along the road . . ."
She smiled, she laughed, her beautiful teeth glowed . . .
"That Laura in the flower of youth! . . . Why, you're
irreverent! . . . You ought to think instead
of my gray hair . . . I don't dye it anymore."

L'onesto rifiuto

    Un mio gioco di sillabe t'illuse.
    Tu verrai nella mia casa deserta:
    lo stuolo accrescerai delle deluse.
    So che sei bella e folle nell'offerta
5 di te. Te stessa, bella preda certa,
    già quasi m'offri nelle palme schiuse.

    Ma prima di conoscerti, con gesto
    franco t'arresto sulle soglie, amica,
    e ti rifiuto come una mendica.
10 Non sono lui, non sono lui! Sí, questo
    voglio gridarti nel rifiuto onesto,
    perché piú tardi tu non maledica.

    Non sono lui! Non quello che t'appaio,
    quello che sogni spirito fraterno!
15 Sotto il verso che sai, tenero e gaio,
    arido è il cuore, stridulo di scherno
    come siliqua stridula d'inverno,
    vôta di semi, pendula al rovaio...

    Per te serbare immune da pensieri
20 bassi, la coscienza ti congeda
    onestamente, in versi piú sinceri...
    Ma (tu sei bella) fa ch'io non ti veda:
    il desiderio della bella preda
    mentirebbe l'amore che tu speri.

The Honest Refusal

One of my games of rhyme led you astray.
You'll enter my empty house, and the whole crew
of your delusions will carry you away.
I know you are beautiful, and crazy too
in the offer of yourself. Already you
with open hands offer me a lovely prey.

Before I know you, before I even allow
you over the threshold, I stop you now, my friend,
refuse you like a beggar's outstretched hand.
I'm not the one! I'm not the one! That's how
I want to shout my honest refusal now,
so you won't come to curse me in the end.

I'm not the one, not the counterpart you need,
the kindred spirit that you dream you see.
Under the light and tender lines you read,
the heart is arid, shrilling its mockery
like a shrilling husk of winter, aimlessly
blown by the north wind, empty, without a seed . . .

To keep you safe from all the thoughts that stir
low in the dark heart, conscience sends you away
in honesty, in verses most sincere . . .
But (you are beautiful) be sure you stay
far from me: hunger for the lovely prey
would wear the mask of the love you hope for here.

25 Non posso amare, Illusa! Non ho amato
mai! Questa è la sciagura che nascondo.
Triste cercai l'amore per il mondo,
triste pellegrinai pel mio passato,
vizioso fanciullo viziato,
30 sull'orme del piacere vagabondo...

Ah! Non volgere i tuoi piccoli piedi
verso l'anima buia di chi tace!
Non mi tentare, pallida seguace!...
Pel tuo sogno, pel sogno che ti diedi,
35 non son colui, non son colui che credi!

Curiosa di me, lasciami in pace!

I cannot love, you fool! I've never loved!
That's the calamity that I conceal.
Sadly I sought the love I'll never feel,
sadly throughout this past of mine I roved,
a child of depravity, a child depraved,
a vagabond who followed pleasure's trail . . .

Don't turn your little feet so trustingly
to find the dark still soul you've never known.
Don't tempt me, pale disciple! . . . For your own
dream, in the name of the dream you had from me,
I'm not the one, not the one you think you see!

My lovely inquisitor, leave me alone!

Torino

I

Quante volte tra i fiori, in terre gaie,
sul mare, tra il cordame dei velieri,
sognavo le tue nevi, i tigli neri,
le dritte vie corrusche di rotaie,
5 l'arguta grazia delle tue crestaie,
o città favorevole ai piaceri!

E quante volte già, nelle mie notti
d'esilio, resupino a cielo aperto,
sognavo sere torinesi, certo
10 ambiente caro a me, certi salotti
beoti assai, pettegoli, bigotti
come ai tempi del buon Re Carlo Alberto...

«... *se 'l Cônt ai ciapa ai rangia për le rime...*»
«*Ch'a staga ciutô...*» – «*'L caso a l'è stupendô!...*»
15 «*E la Duse ci piace?*» – «*Oh! Mi m'antendô
pà vaire... I negô pà, sarà sublime,
ma mi a teatrô i vad për divertime...*»
«*Ch'a staga ciutô!... A jntra 'l Reverendô!...*»

S'avanza un Barnabita, lentamente...
20 stringe la mano alla Contessa amica
siede col gesto di chi benedica...
Ed il poeta, tacito ed assente
si gode quell'accolita di gente
ch'à la tristezza d'una stampa antica...

Turin

I

How many times, in some bright flowery place,
in the cordage of a ship on the high seas,
I've dreamed about your snows, black linden trees,
straight avenues agleam with tracks, your race
of milliners with all their sparkling grace,
city of pleasures, always pleased to please!

And how many times already, as I weathered
nights of exile under a bright clear moon,
I've dreamed of Turin evenings, of the tone
of an atmosphere dear to me, of salons rather
stupid, where bigots and gossipmongers gather
as when good King Carlo Alberto was on the throne . . .

". . . Count catches them, he'll take his revenge in rhyme . . ."
"Be quiet now . . ."—"Say, this house is really grand! . . ."
"D'you like the Duse?"—"Oh, I don't understand
that stuff . . . I'm not denying she's sublime,
but I go to see a show for a good time . . ."
"Be quiet now! . . . Here comes the Reverend! . . ."

Advancing slowly, a Barnabite enters . . . he
presses the hand of the Countess, his dear and loving
friend, and then sits with a gesture as if giving
a blessing . . . And from far off, silently
the poet enjoys that assembled company
that has the sadness of an old engraving . . .

25 Non soffre. Ama quel mondo senza raggio
di bellezza, ove cosa di trastullo
è l'Arte. Ama quei modi e quel linguaggio
e quell'ambiente sconsolato e brullo.
Non soffre. Pensa Giacomo fanciullo
30 e la «siepe» e il «natío borgo selvaggio».

II

Come una stampa antica bavarese
vedo al tramonto il cielo subalpino...
Da Palazzo Madama al Valentino
ardono l'Alpi tra le nubi accese...
35 È questa l'ora *antica* torinese,
è questa l'ora *vera* di Torino...

L'ora ch'io dissi del Risorgimento,
l'ora in cui penso a Massimo d'Azeglio
adolescente, a *I miei ricordi*, e sento
40 d'essere nato troppo tardi... Meglio
vivere al tempo sacro del risveglio,
che al tempo nostro mite e sonnolento!

III

Un po' vecchiotta, provinciale, fresca
tuttavia d'un tal garbo parigino,
45 in te ritrovo me stesso bambino,
ritrovo la mia grazia fanciullesca
e mi sei cara come la fantesca
che m'ha veduto nascere, o Torino!

Tu m'hai veduto nascere, indulgesti
50 ai sogni del fanciullo trasognato:
tutto me stesso, tutto il mio passato,

No pain. He loves that world that's never shone
a ray of beauty, where they make a toy
of Art. He loves those manners and that tone,
and that atmosphere forlorn and bare of joy.
No pain. He thinks of Giacomo as a boy
and the "hedgerow" and the "savage native town."

II

As in an old Bavarian engraving
in the subalpine sky the sun goes down . . .
From Palazzo Madama to the Valentino grounds
between the lighted clouds the Alps are blazing . . .
This is the hour of Turin most worth having,
this is the hour of the true old town . . .

I've talked of the Risorgimento in such hours,
I think of *My Recollections*, of the young
Massimo d'Azeglio, and a feeling overpowers:
I was born too late . . . It was a much finer thing
to live in that sacred reawakening
than in these meek and sleepy days of ours!

III

You're aging a bit, provincial, nonetheless
still fresh with a Parisian courtesy,
and I find the infant that I used to be
in you once more, I find the gracefulness
of childhood once again, and like the nurse
who saw me born, Turin, you're dear to me!

You saw me born, and you indulged all those
dreams of a dreamy little boy: at last
all that I was and am, all of my past,

i miei ricordi piú teneri e mesti
dormono in te, sepolti come vesti
sepolte in un armadio canforato.

55 L'infanzia remotissima... la scuola...
la pubertà... la giovinezza accesa...
i pochi amori pallidi... l'attesa
delusa... il tedio che non ha parola...
la Morte e la mia Musa con sé sola,
60 sdegnosa, taciturna ed incompresa.

IV

Ch'io perseguendo mie chimere vane
pur t'abbandoni e cerchi altro soggiorno,
ch'io pellegrini verso il Mezzogiorno
a belle terre tepide lontane,
65 la metà di me stesso in te rimane
e mi ritrovo ad ogni mio ritorno.

A te ritorno quando si rabbuia
il cuor deluso da mondani fasti.
Tu mi consoli, tu che mi foggiasti
70 quest'anima borghese e chiara e buia
dove ride e singhiozza il tuo Gianduia
che teme gli orizzonti troppo vasti...

Eviva i bôgianen... Sí, dici bene,
o mio savio Gianduia ridarello!
75 Buona è la vita senza foga, bello
goder di cose piccole e serene...

A l'è questiôn d' nen piessla... Dici bene
o mio savio Gianduia ridarello!...

my recollections tender and morose
are sleeping in you, buried here like clothes
left buried in a camphorated chest.

Infancy buried deepest . . . school, and game . . .
my vivid youth . . . the few pale loves I had . . .
all the frustrated waiting that I did . . .
the tedium that doesn't have a name . . .
Death, and my Muse alone where no one came,
disdainful, taciturn, misunderstood.

IV

When I go yonder, deserting you to play
at chasing my chimeras on the run,
when I wander toward the Mezzogiorno sun,
toward lovely lukewarm lands so far away,
half of me stays with you, so that I may
find myself here when I come home again.

I come back home when heart grows dark and drear,
done in by worldly pomp and frippery.
And you console me, you who molded me
into this bourgeois spirit dark and clear
where Punch still laughs and sobs and shows his fear
of the wide horizons stretching endlessly . . .

Long live the stickinthemuds . . . How right you are,
my Punch, so knowing and so quick to laugh!
How lovely is the unimpassioned life,
small and serene, that doesn't venture far . . .

The thing is, don't let it get you . . . Right you are,
my Punch, so knowing and so quick to laugh! . . .

In casa del sopravissuto

I

    Dalle profondità dei cieli tetri
scende la bella neve sonnolenta,
tutte le cose ammanta come spetri;
scende, risale, impetuosa, lenta,
5 di su, di giú, di qua, di là, s'avventa
alle finestre, tamburella i vetri...

    Turbina densa in fiocchi di bambagia,
imbianca i tetti ed i selciati lordi,
piomba dai rami curvi, in blocchi sordi...
10 Nel caminetto crepita la bragia
e l'anima del reduce s'adagia
nella bianca tristezza dei ricordi.

    Reduce dall'Amore e dalla Morte
gli hanno mentito le due cose belle!
15 Gli hanno mentito le due cose belle:
Amore non lo volle in sua coorte,
Morte l'illuse fino alle sue porte,
ma ne respinse l'anima ribelle.

    In braccio ha la compagna: Makakita;
20 e Makakita trema freddolosa,
stringe il poeta e guarda quella cosa
di là dai vetri, guarda sbigottita
quella cosa monotona infinita
che tutto avvolge di bianchezza ondosa.

25   Forse essa pensa i boschi dove nacque,
i tamarindi, i cocchi ed i banani,
il fiume e le sorelle quadrumani,

In the House of the Survivor

I

From the profundity of the dark skies
descends the lovely and the drowsy snow,
cloaking the world in a specterlike disguise:
descends, whips up again, impetuous, slow,
here, there, upward, downward, starts to throw
itself against the windows as it flies . . .

In flakes of cottonwool it swirls around,
whitening all the roofs and filthy streets,
dropping in thudding blocks from the bent trees . . .
In the grate the embers make their crackling sound
and the spirit of the veteran sinks down
in the white sadness of his memories.

A veteran of Love and Death, the two
beautiful things that always told him lies—
Beautiful things that always told him lies:
Love never wanted him among her crew,
Death tantalized him all the way up to
her door, then put the rebel soul to flight.

In his arms is his companion, shivering
Little Magot, who squeezes the poet tight,
shivering with the cold and with her fright,
staring beyond the glass at that strange thing,
staring out at that endless monotonous thing
that wraps the world up in a wave of white.

Perhaps she's thinking of the banana trees,
the tamarinds, the coco palms of home,
the sleepy river, and the favorite game

e il gioco favorito che le piacque,
quando in catena pendula sull'acque
30 stuzzicava le nari dei caimani.

II

Con la Mamma vicina e il cuore in pace,
s'aggira, canticchiando un melodramma;
sospira un po'... Ravviva dalla brace
il guizzo allegro della buona fiamma...
35 Canticchia. E tace con la cara Mamma;
la cara Mamma sa quel che si tace.

Egli s'aggira. Toglie di sul piano-
forte un ritratto: «Quest'effigie!... Mia?...»
E fissa a lungo la fotografia
40 di quel sé stesso già cosí lontano:
«Sí, mi ricordo... Frivolo... mondano...
vent'anni appena... Che malinconia!...

Mah! Come l'*io* trascorso è buffo e pazzo!
Mah...» – «Che sospiri amari! Che rammenti?»
45 «Penso, mammina, che avrò tosto venti-
cinqu'anni! Invecchio! E ancora mi sollazzo
coi versi! È tempo d'essere il ragazzo
piú serio, che vagheggiano i parenti.

Dilegua il sogno d'arte che m'accese;
50 risano a poco a poco, anche di questo!
Lungi dai letterati che detesto,
tra saggie cure e temperate spese,
sia la mia vita piccola e borghese:
c'è in me la stoffa del borghese onesto...»

they played in quadrumanal companies,
when hanging in a chain they used to tease
the nostrils of the caymans in the stream.

II

With his mother near and with his heart in peace,
he roams now, humming an aria from a play.
He sighs a bit . . . And in the fireplace
the merry embers dance their roundelay . . .
He hums. He doesn't have a word to say:
and what he doesn't say, his mother sees.

He roams. He picks up from the piano top
a photograph: "Is that me? . . . Is it really? . . ."
He stares for a long moment at that early
self that was so quickly swallowed up:
"Yes, I remember . . . Frivolous . . . a fop . . .
I was barely twenty then . . . What melancholy! . . .

That past me, so ridiculous, so mad!
Ugh!"—"What's the matter? Why such bitter sighs?"
"Mamma, I'm growing old! Do you realize
I'll soon be twenty-five? Still I fill my pad
with verse! It's time I was that earnest lad
who puts the sparkle into uncles' eyes.

Fled is the dream of art that inflamed my senses:
I feel myself recover more and more.
Far from the literati I abhor,
mid prudent work and moderate expenses,
I'll live my little life without pretenses:
there is in me the stuff of a good bourgeois . . ."

55 Sogghigna un po'. Ricolloca sul pianoforte il ritratto «... Quest'effigie! Mia?...»
E fissa a lungo la fotografia
di quel sé stesso già cosí lontano.
«Un po' malato... frivolo... mondano...
60 Sí, mi ricordo... Che malinconia!...»

He puts the picture on the piano top.
He sneers a bit. ". . . Is that me? Is it really? . . ."
He stares for a long moment at that early
self that was so quickly swallowed up:
"A bit unhealthy . . . frivolous . . . a fop . . .
Yes, I remember him . . . What melancholy! . . ."

Pioggia d'agosto

Nel mio giardino triste ulula il vento,
cade l'acquata a rade goccie, poscia
piú precipite giú crepita scroscia
a fili interminabili d'argento...
5 Guardo la Terra abbeverata e sento
ad ora ad ora un fremito d'angoscia...

Soffro la pena di colui che sa
la sua tristezza vana e senza mete;
l'acqua tessuta dall'immensità
10 chiude il mio sogno come in una rete,
e non so quali voci esili inquete
sorgano dalla mia perplessità.

«La tua perplessità mediti l'ale
verso meta piú vasta e piú remota!
15 È tempo che una fede alta ti scuota,
ti levi sopra te, nell'Ideale!
Guarda gli amici. Ognun palpita quale
demagogo, credente, patriota...

Guarda gli amici. Ognuno già ripose
20 la varia fede nelle varie scuole.
Tu non credi e sogghigni. Or quali cose
darai per meta all'anima che duole?
La Patria? Dio? l'Umanità? Parole
che i retori t'han fatto nauseose!...

August Rain

Wind howls through my sad garden, and the river
of raindrops nearly stops, till suddenly
the downpour roars once more, the sky falls free
in a murmur of interminable threads of silver . . .
I watch the Earth overflowing, and a shiver
of anguish now and then comes over me . . .

I feel the pain of one who knows that he
is suffering vainly and without an aim.
This water woven from the immensity
is closing like a net around my dream,
and I don't know what troubled voices seem
to pipe to me from my perplexity.

"In your perplexity you long to feel
wings for an aim more lofty and profound.
It's time you were shaken, lifted from the ground,
out of yourself, up into the Ideal!
Look at your friends. How all of them throb with zeal,
demagogues, patriots, and the heaven-bound . . .

Look at your friends. How all of them swarm and flush as
they throw themselves into their creeds and missions.
You disbelieve and sneer. Where is the luscious
food for the spirit starving for high ambitions?
Humanity? God? Country? Rhetoricians
have mouthed the words so much they've made them
    nauseous! . . .

25 Lotte brutali d'appetiti avversi
   dove l'anima putre e non s'appaga...
   Chiedi al responso dell'antica maga
   la sola verità buona a sapersi;
   la Natura! Poter chiudere in versi
30 i misteri che svela a chi l'indaga!»

   Ah! La Natura non è sorda e muta;
   se interrogo il lichène ed il macigno
   essa parla del suo fine benigno...
   Nata di sé medesima, assoluta,
35 unica verità non convenuta,
   dinnanzi a lei s'arresta il mio sogghigno.

   Essa conforta di speranze buone
   la giovinezza mia squallida e sola;
   e l'achenio del cardo che s'invola,
40 la selce, l'orbettino, il macaone,
   sono tutti per me come *personæ*,
   hanno tutti per me qualche parola...

   Il cuore che ascoltò, piú non s'acqueta
   in visïoni pallide fugaci,
45 per altre fonti va, per altra meta...
   O mia Musa dolcissima che taci
   allo stridío dei facili seguaci,
   con altra voce tornerò poeta!

The brutal clash of appetites grows worse
as the spirit starves and rots in its distress . . .
You seek an answer from the sorceress—
the one transcendent truth of the universe,
Nature!—to have the power to catch in verse
the mysteries she unveils to those who press."

Ah, Nature isn't deaf, she isn't mute.
If I puzzle the lichen and the sandstone here
she breathes her good intent into my ear . . .
Born of her very self, and absolute,
the only truth that isn't made to suit—
I stand before her and let go my sneer.

In youthful years lived cheerless and alone
she brings me good hopes of the times to be.
The dandelion blown so carelessly,
the swallowtail, the blindworm, and the stone,
each of them has a character of its own,
each of them has some words to say to me . . .

The heart that hears no longer needs the toys
of fleeting dreams and visionary blurs,
but seeks another fount, another choice . . .
O sweetest Muse of mine who never stirs
to the shriekings of the facile followers,
the poet will return with another voice!

I colloqui

I

«I colloqui»... Rifatto agile e sano
aduna i versi, rimaneggia, lima,
bilancia il manoscritto nella mano.

– Pochi giochi di sillaba e di rima:
5 questo rimane dell'età fugace?
È tutta qui la giovinezza prima?

Meglio tacere, dileguare in pace
or che fiorito ancora è il mio giardino,
or che non punta ancora invidia tace.

10 Meglio sostare a mezzo del cammino,
or che il mondo alla mia Musa maldestra,
quasi a mima che canta il suo mattino,

soccorrevole ancor porge la destra.

II

Ma la mia Musa non sarà l'attrice
15 annosa che si trucca e pargoleggia,
e la folla deride l'infelice;

giovine tacerà nella sua reggia,
come quella Contessa Castiglione
bellissima, di cui si favoleggia.

The Colloquies

I

The Colloquies . . . Now strong and spry, remanned,
he gathers the verses, arranges, polishes,
balances the manuscript in his hand.

—Lame games of syllables and rhymes: is this
what's left behind from the time he couldn't keep?
Is it all here, that prime of youthfulness?

Better to fade away without a peep,
now while my garden's still in bloom today,
now while the tongue of envy's still asleep.

Better to stop in the middle of the way,
now while the world still offers in sympathy,
as to the singer warbling her morning lay,

its good right hand to my clumsy Muse and me.

II

My Muse won't be the crumbling prima donna
who paints her face and simpers like a child
and draws the catcalls of the crowd down on her.

She'll retire to her palace undefiled
like the Countess Castiglione, whose beauty made
a legend, and who had the world beguiled.

20 Allo sfiorire della sua stagione,
disparve al mondo, sigillò le porte
della dimora, e ne restò prigione.

Sola col Tempo, tra le stoffe smorte,
attese gli anni, senz'amici, senza
25 specchi, celando al Popolo, alla Corte

l'onta suprema della decadenza.

III

L'immagine di me voglio che sia
sempre ventenne, come in un ritratto;
amici miei, non mi vedrete in via,

30 curvo dagli anni, tremulo e disfatto!
Col mio silenzio resterò l'amico
che vi fu caro, un poco mentecatto;

il fanciullo sarò tenero e antico
che sospirava al raggio delle stelle,
35 che meditava Arturo e Federico,

ma lasciava la pagina ribelle
per seppellir le rondini insepolte,
per dare un'erba alle zampine delle

disperate cetonie capovolte...

Soon as she felt her season start to fade,
she left the world, and sealed inside her grounds
became a prisoner, and there she stayed.

Alone with Time, among her faded gowns,
without a mirror and without a friend,
she met the years, from the Crowd and from the Crowns

hiding the deep disgrace of decadence.

III

I want my image to be always young,
fixed at twenty, as by the artist's hand.
Friends, you won't see me doddering along

bent with the years, hands shaking, all unmanned.
And with my silence I will always be
the friend you loved, a trifle scatterbrained.

I'll stay the tender boy eternally
who looked up at the glowing stars and sighed,
who sifted Arthur and Friedrich's philosophy

but left the rebellious page and went outside
to bury the unburied swallows there,
to extend a blade of grass to the terrified

overturned beetles clawing at the air . . .

from THE ROAD TO SHELTER

(1907)

☆

da LA VIA DEL RIFUGIO

L'analfabeta

Nascere vide tutto ciò che nasce
in una casa, in cinquant'anni. Sposi
novelli, bimbi... I bimbi già corrosi
oggi dagli anni, vide nelle fasce.

5 Passare vide tutto ciò che passa
in una casa, in cinquant'anni. I morti
tutti, egli solo, con le braccia forti
compose lacrimando nella cassa.

Tramonta il giorno, fra le stelle chiare,
10 placido come l'agonia del giusto.
L'ottuagenario candido e robusto
viene alla soglia, con il suo mangiare.

Sorride un poco, siede sulla rotta
panca di quercia; serra per sostegno
15 fra i ginocchi la ciotola di legno:
mangia in pace cosí, mentre che annotta.

Con la barba prolissa come un santo
arissecchito, calvo, con gli orecchi
la fronte coronati di cernecchi
20 il buon servo somiglia il Tempo... Tanto,

tanto simile al Nume pellegrino,
ch'io lo vedo recante nella destra
non la ciotola colma di minestra,
ma la falce corrusca e il polverino.

The Illiterate

He's seen them all, the births of all of those
born in one house in fifty years. New brides
and bridegrooms, babies . . . Babies that the tides
of years have crumbled, he saw in swaddling clothes.

He's seen it all, the march of all that's passed
here in one house in fifty years. The dead
that he with his strong arms and bending head
composed in coffins as the tears came fast.

As peaceful as the dying of the just,
amid the clear white stars, day disappears.
And at the doorstep with his meal appears
the octogenarian honest and robust.

He smiles a bit, and sets himself upon
the wornout oaken bench. Between his knees
he holds his wooden bowl, and thus in peace
he eats his evening meal, as night comes on.

As withered as a saint, and wearing such
a flowing beard, and with his bald head bare,
his brow and ears crowned with stray wisps of hair,
he makes me think of Father Time . . . So much

does he recall a wandering deity
that in his hands it almost seems he has
a gleaming scythe and a huge hourglass
right where the brimming bowl of soup should be.

25 Biancheggia tra le glicini leggiadre
l'umile casa ove ritorno solo.
Il buon custode parla: «O figliuolo,
come somigli al padre di tuo padre!

Ma non amava le città lontane
30 egli che amò la terra e i buoni studi
della terra e la casa che tu schiudi
alla vita per poche settimane...»

Dolce restare! E forza è che prosegua
pel mondo nella sua torbida cura
35 quei che ritorna a questa casa pura
soltanto per concedersi una tregua;

per lungi, lungi riposare gli occhi
(di che riposi parlano le stelle!)
da tutte quelle sciocche donne belle,
40 da tutti quelli cari amici sciocchi...

Oh! il piccolo giardino omai distrutto
dalla gramigna e dal navone folto...
Ascolto il buon silenzio, intento, ascolto
il tonfo malinconico d'un frutto.

45 Si rispecchia nel gran Libro sublime
la mente faticata dalle pagine,
il cuore devastato dall'indagine
sente la voce delle cose prime.

Tramonta il giorno. Un vespero d'oblio
50 riconsola quest'anima bambina;
giunge un riso, laggiú dalla cucina
e il ritmo eguale dell'acciotolio.

The humble house where I've come home alone
amid the wisteria vines looks white and glazed.
The good caretaker speaks: "Son, I'm amazed
how like your father's father you have grown!

But he never loved the cities of the plain.
He loved the good earth and he loved the true
lore of the good earth and this house that you
have briefly opened up to life again . . ."

Sweet repose! It's the force that still pursues
throughout the world through all his restless care
this one who's come home to this pure house where
for now he can allow himself a truce,

can let these eyes rest for a long, long time
(that restfulness of which the clear stars tell)
from all those women stupid and beautiful,
from all those dear and stupid friends of mine . . .

The little garden has been covered up
with weeds and parsnips. With a sharpened ear
I hear the peaceful silence, and I hear
a piece of fruit in a melancholy plop.

The mind ground down by pages can turn here
the leaves of that great Book sublime and vast,
the heart laid waste by inquiry at last
discerns the voice of first things speaking clear.

Day disappears. On this infant soul descends
evening's oblivious blanket. Now already
a laugh comes from the kitchen, and the steady
beat of the clatter of the pots and pans.

In che cortile si lavora il grano?
Sul rombo cupo della trebbiatrice
55 s'innalza un canto giovine che dice:
anche il buon pane – senza sogni – è vano!

Poi tace il grano e la canzone. I greggi
dormono al chiuso. Nella sera pura
indugia il sole: «Or fammi un po' lettura:
60 te beato che sai leggere! Leggi!»

Me beato! Ah! Vorrei ben non sapere
leggere, o Vecchio, le parole d'altri!
Berrei, inconscio di sapori scaltri,
un puro vino dentro il mio bicchiere.

65 E la gioia del canto a me randagio
scintillerebbe come ti scintilla
nella profondità della pupilla
il buon sorriso immune dal contagio.

Gli leggo le notizie del giornale:
70 i casi della guerra non mai sazia
e l'orrore dei popoli che strazia
la gran necessità di farsi male.

Ripensa i giorni dell'armata Sarda,
la guerra di Crimea, egli che seppe
75 la tristezza ai confini delle steppe
e l'assedio nemico che s'attarda.

Poi cade il giorno col silenzio. Poi
rompe il silenzio immobile di tutto
il tonfo malinconico d'un frutto
80 che giunge rotolando sino a noi.

Out in what field are they gathering the grain?
Above the deep throb of the thresher comes
the rhythm of a youthful song that hums:
even the bread—without a dream—is vain!

Then all falls still. The sheep are in the pen,
asleep. The sun hangs in the evening sky,
lingering. "Do me some reading now, my boy.
You're blesséd who know how to read. Read, then!"

Me blesséd! Ah, how I could wish I never
had learned to read the words of other men.
Unconscious of such cunning flavors then,
I'd lift my cup and drink pure wines forever.

And then the joy of the song would bring to my
wandering soul, old fellow, the same peace,
the same deep smile, immune from this disease,
the same delight that sparkles in your eye.

I read him stories from the daily press:
the wars that seas of blood can't satisfy,
the miseries of nations tortured by
the endless need for doing wickedness.

And he recalls once more his days upon
the Russian Steppes with the Sardinian Corps,
the pain and horror of the Crimean War,
the bloody siege that lingered on and on.

Day drops away in silence. Then the sweet
stillness spread over all is broken up
by a piece of fruit in a melancholy plop:
an apple rolls up almost to our feet.

E m'inchino e raccolgo e addento il pomo...
Serenità!... L'orrore della guerra
scende in me: cittadino della Terra,
in me: concittadino d'ogni uomo.

85 Ora il vecchio mi parla d'altre rive
d'altri tempi, di sogni... E piú m'alletta
di tutte, la parola non costretta
di quegli che non sa leggere e scrivere.

Sereno è quando parla e non disprezza
90 il presente pel meglio d'altri tempi:
«O figliuolo il meglio d'altri tempi
non era che la nostra giovinezza!»

Anche dice talvolta, se mi mostro
taciturno: «Tu hai l'anima ingombra.
95 Tutto è fittizio in noi: e Luce ed Ombra:
giova molto foggiarci a modo nostro!

E se l'ombra s'indugia e tu rimuovine
la tristezza. Il dolore non esiste
per chi s'innalza verso l'ora triste
100 con la forza d'un cuore sempre giovine.

Fissa il dolore e armati di lungi,
ché la malinconia, la gran nemica,
si piega inerme, come fa l'ortica
che piú forte l'acciuffi e men ti pungi».

105 E viene allo scrittoio, se m'indugio:
«Ah! Già i capelli ti si fan piú radi,
sei pallido... Da tempo è che non badi
per queste carte al remo e all'archibugio.

I bend and pick it up and bite . . . and in
the quiet, the war's horrors are unfurled
and fall on me, a citizen of the world,
a fellow citizen of every man.

Now the old fellow talks into the night
of other times, of other shores, of dreams . . .
And I'm borne buoyantly on unforced streams
of words from him who cannot read or write.

He speaks serenely, never to dispraise
the present for the best of other times:
"You see, my boy, the best of other times
was nothing, really, but our younger days."

He gathers what my silence seems to say:
"You have a burdened spirit. We are made
of everything unreal, of Light and Shade:
we have to mold ourselves as best we may.

And though the shade may linger, you can drive
away the sadness. Sorrow has no power
over one who rises toward that desperate hour
with a heart still young as long as he's alive.

Stare sorrow in the face: wear battle dress
from far off so that melancholy, your sworn
foe, will submit defenseless, like the thorn
that pricks more deeply but afflicts you less."

He comes to the writing desk where I linger still:
"But how your hair is growing thin, and how
pale you are growing . . . Put these sheets down now:
take up the arquebus, take up the scull.

Chi troppo studia e poi matto diventa!
110 Giova il sapere al corpo che ti langue?
Vale ben meglio un'oncia di buon sangue
che tutta la saggezza sonnolenta».

Cosí ragiona quegli che non crede
la troppo umana favola d'un Dio,
115 che rinnegò la chiesa dell'oblio
per la necessità d'un'altra fede.

Dice: «Ritorna il fiore e la bisavola.
Tutto ritorna vita e vita in polve:
ritorneremo, poiché tutto evolve
120 nella vicenda d'un'eterna favola».

Ma come, o Vecchio, un giorno fu distrutto
il sogno della tua mente fanciulla?
E chi ti apprese la parola *nulla*,
e chi ti apprese la parola *tutto*?

125 Certo, fissando un cielo puro, un fiume
antico, meditando nello specchio
dell'acque e delle nubi erranti, il Vecchio
lesse i misteri, come in un volume.

Come dal tutto si rinnovi in cellula
130 tutto; e la vita spenta dei cadaveri
risusciti le selve ed i papaveri
e l'ingegno dell'uomo e la libellula.

Come una legge senza fine domini
le cose nate per se stesse, eterne...
135 Tanto discerne quei che non discerne
i segni convenuti dagli uomini.

Study too much and soon you'll fry your brains.
What's learning when the body starts to fall?
Better one ounce of good red blood than all
the drowsy wisdom that the world contains."

He reasons thus who puts no credence in
the all too human fable of a God,
who in the hunger for another creed
renounced the credo of oblivion.

"The flower and the ancestor are able
to come back. All comes back, all turns to dust.
We'll come back. Everything, just as it must,
evolves in the whirling of an eternal fable."

How was it that one day it died from you,
the dream to which your childlike mind could cling?
And who taught you the word for *everything*,
and who taught you the word for *nothing* too?

Gazing upon a pure sky, casting a look
on an ancient river, meditating on
a mirror of water or drifting clouds, the old man
has read the mysteries, as in a book.

How from the All, cells re-create the All,
and how the spent life of cadavers can
reanimate the woods, the mind of man,
the mayfly, and all creatures great and small.

How things born of themselves are subject to
the eternal sway of a law without an end . . .
He comprehends this, who can't comprehend
the symbols man has given meaning to.

Ma come cadde la tua fede illesa:
fede ristoratrice d'ogni piaga
per l'anima fanciulla che s'appaga
140 nei simulacri della Santa Chiesa?

Come vedi le cose? Senza fedi,
stanco, sul limitare della morte,
sai vivere sereno, o vecchio forte,
sorridere pacato... Come vedi?

145 Guardi le stelle attingere i fastigi
dell'abetaia, contro il cielo, e l'orsa
volger le sette gemme alla sua corsa:
senti il ritmo macàbro delle strigi

e il frullo della nottola ed il frullo
150 della falena... Pel sereno illune
spazi tranquillo, vecchio saggio immune.
La tua pupilla è quella d'un fanciullo.

Qualche cosa tu vedi che non vedo
in quell'immensità, con gli occhi puri:
155 «Buona è la morte» dici e t'avventuri
serenamente al prossimo congedo.

Ancora sento al tuo cospetto il simbolo
d'una saggezza mistica e solenne;
quello mi tiene ancora che mi tenne
160 strano mistero, di quand'ero bimbo.

Allora che su questa soglia stessa
mi narravi di guerre e d'altri popoli,
dicevi del Mar Nero e Sebastopoli,
dei Turchi, di Lamarmora, d'Odessa.

But how did your faith fall down unharmed—that creed
in which the childlike soul fulfills its search
as the simulacra of Holy Mother Church
heal every scar and answer every need?

How do you see things? Sitting patiently
at death's door, tired, without a faith, you know
the way to live serenely, and you show
a smile of calm acceptance . . . How do you see?

You watch the rising stars as they appear
above the highest firs, against the sky,
you watch the Great Bear as she wanders by
turning the seven jewels, and you hear

the haunted rhythm of the screech-owls' cry,
the whirr of bat wings . . . Through the moonless shade
you wander sagely, calm and unafraid.
You look out at the world through a child's eye.

You look into the vast expanse of night
and you see something there that I can't see.
"It's good to die," you say: in serenity
you walk into the dying of the light.

And in your presence I can sense once more
the emblem of a mystic and profound
wisdom, whose strangest spell has once more found
the boy it found so many years before.

Here on this very doorstep you'd unroll
your tales of war and alien lands to me,
of Odessa and the Turks and the Black Sea,
of Lamarmora and Sebastopol.

165 E nel mio sogno s'accendean le vampe
sopra le mura. Entrava la milizia
nella città: una città fittizia
quali si vedon nelle vecchie stampe,

le vecchie stampe incorniciate in nero:
170 ...i panorami di Gerusalemme,
il Gran Sultano, carico di gemme...:
artificiose, belle piú del vero;

le vecchie stampe, care ai nostri nonni
...il minareto e tre colonne infrante,
175 il mare, la galea, il mercatante...
città vedute nei miei primi sonni.

Ed ora, o vecchio, e sazi la tua fame
sulla panca di quercia, ove m'indugio;
altro sentiero tenta al suo rifugio
180 il bimbo illuso dalle stampe in rame.

And in my dream flames roared above the ravings
of those within the walls, and the militia
marched into the city: an artificial
city just like the ones in old engravings,

those old engravings that we used to see
in black frames: the Grand Sultan decked with gems,
and the panoramas of Jerusalem . . . ,
mannered, more lovely than reality . . .

those old engravings from grandfather's days
. . . the city walls, the minaret and three
smashed columns, galley and merchantman on the sea . . .
city that set my earliest dreams ablaze.

On the oak bench, where I linger now, your cravings
have been satisfied by that wooden bowl of yours.
Another pathway with its shelter lures
the boy beguiled by copperplate engravings.

La differenza

Penso e ripenso: – Che mai pensa l'oca
gracidante alla riva del canale?
Pare felice! Al vespero invernale
protende il collo, giubilando roca.

5 Salta starnazza si rituffa gioca:
né certo sogna d'essere mortale
né certo sogna il prossimo Natale
né l'armi coruscanti della cuoca.

– O pàpera, mia candida sorella,
10 tu insegni che la Morte non esiste:
solo si muore da che s'è pensato.

Ma tu non pensi. La tua sorte è bella!
Ché l'esser cucinato non è triste,
triste è il pensare d'esser cucinato.

The Difference

I think and think again: —What thought provokes
the honking goose on the bank of the canal?
She seems happy! Winter twilight starts to fall:
she stretches her neck and jubilantly croaks.

She scampers flaps her feathers dives and jokes:
she doesn't dream she's a dying animal,
she doesn't dream of the Christmas feast and all
the cook's cold weapons and their gleaming strokes.

—Gosling, untainted sister, you signify
there's no such thing as Death. And I agree:
we start to think and then we start to die.

But you don't think. A happier destiny!
That we will fry is no great tragedy:
what's tragic is the thinking that we'll fry.

Parabola

Il bimbo guarda fra le dieci dita
la bella mela che vi tiene stretta;
e indugia – tanto è lucida e perfetta –
a dar coi denti quella gran ferita.

5 Ma dato il morso primo ecco s'affretta:
e quel che morde par cosa scipita
per l'occhio intento al morso che l'aspetta...
E già la mela è per metà finita.

Il bimbo morde ancora – e ad ogni morso
10 sempre è lo sguardo che precede il dente –
fin che s'arresta al torso che già tocca.

«Non sentii quasi il gusto e giungo al torso!»
Pensa il bambino... Le pupille intente
ogni piacere tolsero alla bocca.

Parable

Through tiny fingers he looks to see
the happy apple he clutches tight:
he waits—it's perfect and so bright—
before he inflicts the injury.

He hurries once he starts to bite:
now the apple sits insipidly
in the eye ambitious for delight . . .
Already it's half what it used to be.

He bites and then he bites some more—
each time the look before the tooth—
until he stops when the core arrives.

"Hardly a taste and here's the core!"
the boy thinks . . . The ambitious eyes
have pulled each pleasure to the mouth.

L'intruso

Le tre sorelle dalla tela rozza
levano gli occhi sbigottite, poi
che una voce pervade i corridoi
come d'uno che irride o che singhiozza.

5 «Il vento in casa!» Il vento cresce, cozza,
sibila, mugge come cento buoi.
Ogni sorella pensa ai casi suoi,
l'altra chiamando con la voce mozza.

In breve dai soppalchi al limitare
10 discacciano il nemico, nell'assedio
invocando a gran voce tutti i Santi.

Ognuna torna poi ad agucchiare,
ed accompagna il ritmo del suo tedio
all'orchestra dei tremoli svettanti.

The Intruder

Terrified eyes arising from the heaps
of rough cloth, the three sisters hear the roars
of a mighty voice that fills the corridors
like one who laughs in scorn or madly weeps.

"The wind is in the house!" It crashes, leaps,
whistles, and bellows like a hundred steers.
Each concentrates upon her own affairs,
calling the others with choked-off little peeps.

Down from the attic, right out the front door
they chase the foe, and till the siege is through
they call on all the Saints with booming pleas.

Then they take up their sewing things once more
and rock the rhythm of their boredom to
the orchestra of the lopped poplar trees.

La forza

A Mario B., lottatore

Bestialità divina, amico Mario,
quando affatichi i muscoli ben atti
e cingi e premi, ansando, e scuoti a tratti
il torso dell'atletico avversario!

5 Bene sai l'arte della forza. In vario
modo lo spossi e incalzi e pieghi e abbatti;
ti sussulta nei muscoli contratti
non so che desiderio sanguinario.

Gràvagli sopra, crudelmente bello,
10 con le scapole fa ch'egli riverso
tocchi la rena e «vinto» gli si gridi!

Ridevole miseria d'un cervello,
quando il proteso già pollice verso
«Uccidi – griderei – Uccidi! Uccidi!»

Strength

To Mario B., wrestler

Blest bestiality, Mario my buddy,
when you play out those highly polished muscles
and grip him, panting, in one of those great tussles
and seize, ease, squeeze, until he turns to putty.

Master of arts of strength, how well you study
to tire, trap, tear him down to his corpuscles,
while tingling through your rippling muscles rustles
some lust that I don't know, so wholly bloody.

Now fall down on him like a monolith
ruthlessly lovely, shoulder him to the ground
till he touches the sand, cries "uncle" and lies still.

Ridiculous misery of a brain, when with
thumbs down already flashed and the winner crowned,
"Kill!"—I would shout and scream it out—"Kill! Kill!"

Un rimorso

I

O il tetro Palazzo Madama...
la sera... la folla che imbruna...
Rivedo la povera cosa,

la povera cosa che m'ama:
5 la tanto simile ad una
piccola attrice famosa.

Ricordo. Sul labbro contratto
la voce a pena s'udí:
«O Guido! Che cosa t'ho fatto
10 di male per farmi cosí?»

II

Sperando che fosse deserto
varcammo l'androne, ma sotto
le arcate sostavano coppie

d'amanti... Fuggimmo all'aperto:
15 le cadde il bel manicotto
adorno di mammole doppie.

O noto profumo disfatto
di mammole e di *petit-gris*...
«Ma Guido, che cosa t'ho fatto
20 di male per farmi cosí?»

Remorse

I

Evening . . . the gloomy Palazzo
Madama . . . the darkening flocks
of people . . . I see her, yes,

the poor little thing I've got so
in love with me, who looks
like a famous little actress.

Tight lips, voice woebegone,
I still can hear her say:
"O Guido! What have I done
for you to treat me this way?"

II

Hoping no one was about
we crossed the hall: we found
the arcade filled up with sets

of lovers . . . We hurried out:
the pretty muff fell to the ground
with its double violets.

The well-known perfume undone
by violets and *petit-gris* . . .
"But Guido, what have I done
for you to treat me this way?"

III

Il tempo che vince non vinca
la voce con che mi rimordi,
o bionda povera cosa!

Nell'occhio azzurro pervinca,
25 nel piccolo corpo ricordi
la piccola attrice famosa...

Alzò la *veletta*. S'udí
(o misera tanto nell'atto!)
ancora: «Che male t'ho fatto,
30 o Guido, per farmi cosí?»

IV

Varcammo di tra le rotaie
la Piazza Castello, nel viso
sferzati dal gelo piú vivo.

Passavano giovani gaie...
35 Avevo un cattivo sorriso:
eppure non sono cattivo,

non sono cattivo, se qui
mi piange nel cuore disfatto
la voce: «Che male t'ho fatto
40 o Guido per farmi cosí?»

III

Conquering time doesn't conquer
the voice that pricks me still,
poor little fair-haired miss.

With your eyes of periwinkle
and small body, you recall
the famous little actress . . .

She raised her *voilette*. At the play
(as mournful now as then)
I could hear: "But what have I done,
O Guido, to treat me this way?"

IV

Over the tracks we crossed
the Piazza Castello, while
the cold made our faces glow.

Laughing young people went past . . .
I was wearing a villainous smile:
and yet I'm no villain, no,

I'm no villain, if I can say
that the heart is still undone
by that voice: "What have I done,
O Guido, to treat me this way?"

L'ultima rinunzia

«... l'una a soffrire e l'altro a far soffrire»

I

– «O Poeta, la tua mamma
che ti diede vita e latte,
che le guancie s'è disfatte
nel cantarti ninna-nanna,

5 lei che non si disfamò,
perché tu ti disfamassi,
lei che non si dissetò,
perché tu ti dissetassi,

la tua madre ha fame, tanta
10 fame! E cade per fatica,
s'accontenta d'una mica;
tu soccorri quella santa!

Ella ha sete! Né t'incresca
di portarle tu da bere:
15 s'accontenta d'un bicchiere,
d'un bicchiere d'acqua fresca».

– «Perché sali alle mie celle?
Che mi ciarli, che mi ciarli?
Non concedo mi si parli
20 quando parlo con le Stelle.

Mamma ha fame? E vada al tozzo
e potrà ben disfamarsi.
Mamma ha sete? E vada al pozzo
e potrà ben dissetarsi.

The Last Renunciation

> ". . . the one to suffer, the other to make her suffer"

I

—"O Poet, your mamma who
gave you life and gave you suck,
and who wore away her cheeks
singing lullabies for you,

she who wouldn't touch a crust
so that you would be fed first,
she who sat as parched as dust
so that you could quench your thirst,

now she's just about to faint!
How the hunger pains attack her!
Yet she hardly takes a cracker.
You must run and help that saint!

She's so thirsty! Shake a leg
(you won't mind), go get a beaker:
she just sips, while growing weaker,
some warm water from the jug."

—"Who's come up my tower stairs?
What's this gabbing, all this gabbing?
I can't bother with this crabbing
while I'm talking with the Stars.

Mamma's hungry? Then go get her
day-old bread: that ought to do.
Mamma's thirsty? Then you'd better
fetch a pail of water too.

25 O s'affacci al limitare,
si rivolga alla comare:
ma lasciatemi sognare,
ma lasciatemi sognare!»

II

– «O Poeta, la tua mamma
30 che ti diede vita e latte,
che le guancie s'è disfatte
nel cantarti ninna-nanna,

la tua mamma che quand'eri
ammalato t'assisteva,
35 non mangiava, non beveva
nei tristissimi pensieri,

lei che t'era sempre intorno
per rifarti sano e forte
per contenderti alla Morte,
40 e piangeva, e notte e giorno

invocava Gesú Cristo
e la Vergine Maria:
o Poeta! ed oggi ho visto
la tua madre in agonia!

45 Oh! l'atroce dipartita!
Chinerai la testa bionda
sulla fronte incanutita
della santa moribonda?»

Now go out the way you came,
get some friends in on your scheme:
go away and let me dream,
go away and let me dream!"

II

—"O Poet, your mamma who
gave you life and gave you suck,
and who wore away her cheeks
singing lullabies for you,

who when you were nearly dying
sat and rubbed your little feet,
couldn't drink and couldn't eat,
so sadly was she sighing,

and who fought with all her might
against Death, to keep you in it,
never left your side a minute,
cried a stream, and day and night

called out to Heaven's Queen
and Christ in his charity:
O Poet! today I've seen
your mother's last agony!

How she writhes and moans! It's horrid!
Won't you lay your curly head
on that holy withered forehead
one more time before she's dead?"

– «Taciturna è la fortuna.
50 Che mi ciarli, che mi ciarli?
Non concedo mi si parli
quando parlo con la Luna!

Forse che dallo speziale
non c'è benda e medicina?
55 Forse che nel casolare
non c'è Ghita la vicina?

La vicina a confortare,
medicina a risanare:
ma lasciatemi sognare,
60 ma lasciatemi sognare!»

III

– «O Poeta, la tua mamma
che ti diede vita e latte,
che le guancie s'è disfatte
nel cantarti ninna-nanna,

65 – odi, anco se t'annoia! –
lei che t'ebbe come un sole,
che t'apprese le parole
che ora sono la tua gioia,

la tua mamma in sulla porta
70 fu trovata sola e morta!
Sola e morta chi sa come
singhiozzando nel tuo nome...

—"Who can make out Fate's tune?
What's this gabbing, all this gabbing?
I can't bother with this crabbing
while I'm talking with the Moon.

Don't they carry pills and ointment
at the chemist's anymore?
And unless they have an appointment
aren't the people home next door?

They'll help her get back on the beam,
the tonic'll bring back her gleam:
go away and let me dream,
go away and let me dream!"

III

—"O Poet, your mamma who
gave you life and gave you suck,
and who wore away her cheeks
singing lullabies for you,

—yes, you're bored, but one thing more—
she to whom you were a sun,
she who taught you one by one
all those words you're crazy for,

your mamma was found, alone
in her doorway, dead as a stone!
Dead who knows how, and crying
out your name as she lay dying . . .

Vieni a piangere la cara,
prima che altri le ritocchi
75 giú le palpebre sugli occhi
e la metta nella bara.

Son le donne già raccolte
là, nell'opera funesta:
ma tu chiamala tre volte
80 s'ella vuol che tu la vesta».

— «Che mi dici, che mi dici,
che mi parli tu di lutto?
Non intendo ciò che dici
quando parlo con il Tutto.

85 Forse che lamentatrici
non ci sono a lamentare?
Forse che becchini e preti
non ci sono a sotterrare?

E la fate lamentare
90 e la fate sotterrare:
ma lasciatemi sognare,
ma lasciatemi sognare!

Ma lasciatemi sognare!»

Come and weep beside her bed,
come before the undertaker
and his underlings remake her
and they seal the coffin lid.

For the sad work still to do
the women already gather:
call her name three times if you
are the one she wished to clothe her."

—"What's this braying, all this braying
calling me to mourn and bawl?
I don't hear a word you're saying
while I'm talking with the All.

For the mourning and the praying
aren't there mourners by the ream?
Aren't gravediggers there waiting
and the priest to sound the theme?

That's enough to make a team,
that's enough to weep a stream:
go away and let me dream,
go away and let me dream!

Go away and let me dream!"

UNCOLLECTED POEMS
☆
POESIE SPARSE

Parabola dei frutti

> Ecce Ancilla Domini.
> Fiat mihi secundum verbum tuum.
> (Salmo dell'Immacolata Concezione).

Il volto un poco inchina
– né triste né giocondo –
sopra il seno infecondo
la Donna sibillina.

5 Il piucheumano mesto
volto sacerdotale
l'assembra una vestale
senza parola e gesto.

Da lunga data tiene
10 i frutti contro il seno,
né i polsi vengon meno
nella fatica lene.

Ardon di pari ardore
i frutti della Terra
15 ch'Ella commisti serra
con quelli dell'Amore.

E nel suo cuore ascoso
un brivido la scuote:
pensa dolcezze ignote
20 in braccio dello Sposo.

Quando l'Annunciatore
verrà nel suo conspetto
recando il bacio e il detto
del dolce suo Signore,

Parable of the Fruit

> *Ecce Ancilla Domini.*
> *Fiat mihi secundum verbum tuum.*
> (Psalm of the Immaculate Conception)

Her face drawn down a bit
—not joyful nor distressed—
over her barren breast,
the sibylline Lady sits.

The morethanhuman sad
and sacerdotal face
calls up a vestal's grace
without a word or deed.

For long she's held the fruit
against her unfulfilled
breast, her pulse unstilled
in a mellow lassitude.

The fruits of the earth that she
is pressing close to these
same fruits of love are seized
with the same intensity.

And in heart's secret place
a shiver takes her as
she thinks of unknown joys
in her Husband's sweet embrace.

And when the Messenger,
the bringer of the word
and the kiss of her sweet Lord,
has come at last to her,

25 allor su l'origliere
   per Lui tutti disserra
   e i frutti della Terra
   e i frutti del Piacere.

then on her pillow she
for Him will disclose all:
the fruits of the earth and all
the fruits of ecstasy.

«Demi-vierge»

per A. J. H.

I

Non ti conobbi mai. Ti riconosco.
Perché già vissi; e quando fui ministro
d'un rito osceno, agitator di sistro
t'ho posseduta al limite d'un bosco.

5 Bene ravviso il sopracciglio fosco
le bande fulve... Chi segnò di bistro
l'occhio caprino gelido sinistro?
Or ti rivedo in un giardino tosco,

vergine impura, dopo mille e mille
10 anni d'esilio. Tu, fatta Britanna,
scendi in Italia a ricercarvi il sogno.

Sono tre mila anni che t'agogno!
Ma com'è lungi il sogno che m'affanna!
Dove sono la tunica e le armille?

II

Dove sono la tunica e le armille
d'elettro che portavi a Siracusa?
E le fontane e i templi d'Aretusa
e l'erme e gli oleandri delle ville?

Demi-vierge

for A.f.H.

I

I never knew you. I recognize you now.
I've lived before, and when I was a priest
shaking my sistrum at an obscene feast
I had you in the forest, under a bough.

How well I recollect the shaded brow,
the bands of tawny hair . . . But who has creased
those glittering goatish eyes with bistre-grease?
I meet you in a Tuscan garden now,

unchaste virgin, after the thousands of long
years of exile. You've come to Italy
in British form, to seek the dream you knew.

For these three thousand years I've wanted you!
But how far is the dream that eats at me.
Where are the tunic and the armlets gone?

II

Where are the tunic and the armlets, where
are the clothes you wore at Syracuse that day?
And the Arethusan temples, the fountains' spray,
and the herms, and the oleander in the air?

5 Del tempo ti restò nelle pupille
soltanto la lussuria che t'accusa,
vergine impura dalla fronte chiusa
tra le due bande lucide e tranquille.

E questa sera tu lasci le danze
10 (per quel ricordo al limite d'un bosco?)
tutta fremendo, come un'arpa viva.

Giungono i suoni dalle aperte stanze
fin nel giardino... O bocca! Riconosco
bene il profumo della tua genciva!

All that has stayed with you from those moments there
is the wantonness in your eyes. It gives you away,
unchaste virgin with forehead hidden away
under two calm and shining bands of hair.

You walked away this evening from the ball
(for the memory of that time beneath the bough?)
and like a living harp you're quivering.

From the open rooms the melodies softly fall
here in the garden . . . And now your mouth, and now
how I recognize the perfume that it brings!

Il modello

Perché non tenteremo la fortuna
d'un bel sonetto biascicante in *ore*
e dove il core rimi con amore
e dove luna rimi con laguna?
5 Pensiero! – E non bellezza inopportuna.
Sincerità! – Il tema delle «otto ore».
Amore! – Un tal che si trapassa il core
per una sarta, al chiaro della luna.

«Ma che arte, che lima!... Chi s'adopra,
10 scrivendo, a farsi intendere con poca
fatica, sarà valido e sincero...»

Cosí farò. Cosí, lasciata l'opra
del paiolo e del mestolo, la cuoca
dirà con te: «Ma qui c'è del pensiero!»

The Pattern

Why don't we try out luck this afternoon
with a lovely sonnet mumbling from the start,
the kind where you rhyme "heart" with "never part,"
the kind where you rhyme "moon" with "old lagoon"?

Sincerity!—"Eight-hour day" will be our tune.
Deep thought!—And not unseasonable art.
Love!—The kind that cuts right through the heart
like a dressmaker, by the light of the moon.

"What skill, what finish! A writer who really works
to make himself understood with a minimum
of effort, he's an artist, he's sincere . . ."

That's how I'll do it. That way, leaving the works
of the kettle and the ladle, cook'll come
and say with you: "Real food for thought, this here!"

«*Historia*»

E l'anno scorso è morta.
Ebbe un amante. Pare.

Ricordi? Io la rivedo,
rivedo la compagna,
5 la classe, la lavagna,
e lei china alla filza
dei verbi greci... Smilza
e mascula: un cinedo
molto ricciuto e bello...
10 Ricordi? Io la rivedo
bionda, sciocchina, gaia:
un piccolo cervello
poco intellettuale
di piccola crestaia
15 molto sentimentale.
Non la ricordi? Smorta,
con certe iridi chiare
dal vasto arco ciliare...

E l'anno scorso è morta.
20 Ebbe un amante. Pare.

Quella è la casa dove
crebbe fanciulla. Guarda
quella finestra dove
vegliava ad ora tarda;
25 il biondo capo chino
su pergamene rozze
di greco e di latino,
sugli assiomi nudi...
Ma poi lascia gli studi

Historia

And just last year she died.
It seems she had a lover.

Remember? I see her again,
I see the class, the slate,
I see the little classmate
bending over a string
of Greek verbs . . . A tiny thing,
curly-haired and thin,
her body boyishly slight . . .
Remember? I see her again
merry and blonde, a little
silly, not very bright,
that little brain of hers
so very like a little
sentimental milliner's.
Don't you remember her? Wide
clear eyes, the whiteness of her,
thick lashes, how they'd hover . . .

And just last year she died.
It seems she had a lover.

That's the house right there
where she grew up, and right
there is the window where
she'd sit up late at night,
her blonde head bending over
scratchy parchments full
of Greek and Latin, over
plain axioms . . . But then
she left all the masculine

30 maschi, passando a nozze
cospicue: un amico,
pare, un amico antico
della madre, uno sposo
ricchissimo ed annoso,
35 inglese, che la porta
in terra d'oltremare...

E l'anno scorso è morta.
Ebbe un amante. Pare.

Volsero gli anni. Ed ella
40 esule sul Tamigi
non dava piú novella...
Pure, nei giorni grigi,
tra i miei grigi ricordi,
vedevo a quando a quando
45 i coniugi discordi:
lo sposo venerando
e l'esile compagna
signora in Gran Bretagna...

Quand'ecco fa ritorno
50 fra noi, senza marito;
e fu rivista un giorno
piú bella nel vestito
cupo... Cercava intorno
col volto sbigottito,
55 con la pupilla assorta,
chi la volesse amare...

E l'anno scorso è morta.
Ebbe un amante. Pare.

books. What a notable
wedding it was: a friend,
it seems, a very old friend
of her mother's, a very old
husband with plenty of gold,
English, who took his bride
to live by London's river . . .

And just last year she died.
It seems she had a lover.

The years went by. And from
the exile so far away
no news would ever come . . .
And yet, when days were gray,
in my gray memories, there
I'd see them now and then,
that so discordant pair:
the venerable man
and his slim mate—her life
in Britain, as his wife . . .

Suddenly she came back,
alone, among us once more,
wearing a dress of black,
lovelier than before . . .
And all around she'd look,
her face dismayed and sore,
her eyes absorbed and wide,
for someone who would love her . . .

And just last year she died.
It seems she had a lover.

[*Stecchetti*]

Perché dalla tua favola compianta –
Renzo Stecchetti, musa prediletta
dello scolaro e della feminetta –
resuscita un passato che m'incanta?

5 Tu mi ricordi l'ottocento e ottanta
mi ricordi la mamma giovinetta
che ti rilegge e ti ripone in fretta;
e intorno un maggio antico odora e canta.

Per quel passato, pel destino bieco
10 tu mi sei caro, finto morituro
che piangi e imprechi e gemi nello strazio.

Io non gemo, fratello, e non impreco:
scendo ridendo verso il fiume oscuro
che ci affranca dal Tempo e dallo Spazio.

[Stecchetti]

I wonder why your dead and gone romancing—
Renzo Stecchetti, every line still weighty
to the schoolboy and the pretty little lady—
reanimates a past that's so entrancing.

You raise for me the days of 1880
and a girl (my mother) reading you and glancing
nervously, hiding you hurriedly: and already
an antique April sets the air to dancing.

For that past, for the doom you made your own
you're dear to me. Like the dying man you weren't,
you moaned and wept and tore your hair in rhyme.

But, brother, I don't weep and I don't moan.
I go down laughing toward that murky current
that liberates us out of Space and Time.

La piú bella

I

Ma bella piú di tutte l'Isola Non-Trovata:
quella che il Re di Spagna s'ebbe da suo cugino
il Re di Portogallo con firma sugellata
e bulla del Pontefice in gotico latino.

5 L'Infante fece vela pel regno favoloso,
vide le Fortunate: Iunonia, Gorgo, Hera
e il Mare di Sargasso e il Mare Tenebroso
quell'isola cercando... Ma l'isola non c'era.

Invano le galee panciute a vele tonde,
10 le caravelle invano armarono la prora:
con pace del Pontefice l'isola si nasconde,
e Portogallo e Spagna la cercano tuttora.

II

L'isola esiste. Appare talora di lontano
tra Teneriffe e Palma, soffusa di mistero:
15 «... l'Isola Non-Trovata!» Il buon Canarïano
dal Picco alto di Teyde l'addita al forestiero.

La segnano le carte antiche dei corsari.
... Hiſola da – trovarſi?... Hiſola pellegrina?...
È l'isola fatata che scivola sui mari;
20 talora i naviganti la vedono vicina...

The Loveliest

I

But the Undiscovered Island's the loveliest of all,
the island that was ceded to the Spanish King
with the royal seal of his kinsman the King of Portugal
and a papal bull in Latin with Gothic lettering.

The Infante's fleet set sail for that fabulous empery,
he saw the Fortunate Isles, he saw wonders everywhere,
he saw the Sea of Darkness and the wide Sargasso Sea,
searching for that island . . . But the island wasn't there.

In vain the caravels with prows to slice the spray,
the galleons bulging vainly with every swollen sail:
with the papal peace the island hid itself away,
and Portugal and Spain go searching for it still.

II

The island exists. She appears in the distance now and then
between Tenerife and Palma, veiled in mystery:
". . . The Undiscovered Island!" The good Canaryman
atop Teide points her out to the man from across the sea.

The corsairs marked her on the maps of other days:
. . . Islande of—where to fix it? . . . Islande of wand'ring
   lande? . . .
She's the enchanted island that glides across the waves,
and now and then the sailors see her close at hand . . .

Radono con le prore quella beata riva:
tra fiori mai veduti svettano palme somme,
odora la divina foresta spessa e viva,
lacrima il cardamomo, trasudano le gomme...

25 S'annuncia col profumo, come una cortigiana,
l'Isola Non-Trovata... Ma, se il piloto avanza,
rapida si dilegua come parvenza vana,
si tinge dell'azzurro color di lontananza...

Sometimes with their prows they graze that blessed shore:
from the dense breathing forest a heavenly fragrance seeps,
between unimagined flowers the swaying palm trees soar,
the rubber trees perspire, the cardamom plant weeps . . .

She lures them with her perfume, like a courtesan,
the Undiscovered Island . . . But if they come her way,
rapidly she'll vanish like a vision on the wind,
hiding herself in the azure colors of faraway . . .

Le non godute

Desiderate piú delle devote
che lasceremmo già senza rimpianti,
amiche alcune delle nostre amanti,
altre note per nome ed altre ignote
5 passano, ai nostri giorni, con il viso
seminascosto dal cappello enorme,
svegliando il desiderïo che dorme
col baleno degli occhi e del sorriso.

E l'affanno sottile non ci lascia
10 tregua; ma piú si intorbida e si affina
idealmente dentro la guaina
morbida della veste che le fascia...
Desiderate e non godute – ancora
nessuna prova ci deluse – alcune
15 serbano come una purezza immune
dalla folla che passa e che le sfiora.

Altre, consunte, taciturne, assorte
guardano e non sorridono: ma sembra
che la profferta delle belle membra
20 renda l'Amore simile alla Morte;
ardenti tutte d'una febbre e cieche
di vanità; biondissime, d'un biondo
oro, le cinge il pettine, secondo
l'antica foggia delle donne greche.

25 Per altre, il nodo greve dell'oscura
treccia è d'insostenibile tormento;
sembra che il collo, esile troppo, a stento,
sorregga il peso dell'acconciatura;

The Unenjoyed

Desired more than those clinging devotees
we would leave without a moment of regret,
some known by name and some we never met,
others friends of our mistresses, through our days
they pass us by with faces all the while
half hidden by huge hats, and still they keep
arousing the desire that lies asleep
with the flashing of their eyes and a flashing smile.

This fine affliction leaves no breathing spell,
to more and more of a turbid density
it gathers, and it's refined ideally
in the soft sheath of a dress that clings so well . . .
Desired and unenjoyed—still we don't try,
we've never been deflated by a test—
some like an icon hold back unpossessed
by the crowd that grazes as it passes by.

Others, worn out already, taciturn,
watch us and never smile, and yet it seems
that in the tender of their lovely limbs
they render Love too much like Death: they burn
with fever and they're blind with vanity,
the blondest and the fairest, blonde as gold:
comb gathers up their hair as in the old
fashion of a Greece that used to be.

For others, it's just too much to endure
that dark and heavy knot: the neck is too
slender for all the work it has to do,
bearing the burden of the thick coiffure.

l'opera dei veleni in altre adempie
30 un prodigio purpureo: le chiome
splendono di riflessi senza nome
dilatandosi ai lati delle tempie...

Belle promesse inutili d'un bene
lusingatore della nostra brama,
35 quando una sola donna che non s'ama
c'incatena con tutte le catene;
quando ogni giorno l'anima delusa
sente che sfugge il meglio della vita,
come sfugge la sabbia tra le dita
40 stretta nel cavo della mano chiusa...

Le incontrammo dovunque: nelle sere
di teatro, alla luce che c'illude;
la bella curva delle spalle ignude
ci avvinse del suo magico potere;
45 e quando l'ombra si abbatté su loro
addensandosi cupa entro le file
dei palchi, il freddo lampo d'un monile
fu l'indice del duplice tesoro.

E le avemmo compagne, ma per brevi
50 ore, in vïaggi taciti, in ritorni,
le ritrovammo dopo pochi giorni
nei rifugi dell'Alpi, tra le nevi;
le ritrovammo sulla spiaggia, al mare,
dove la brama ci ferí piú acuta:
55 ah! Per quella signora sconosciuta
ore insonni, alla notte, lungo il mare!...

Chi sono e dove vanno? Dove vanno
le crëature nomadi? Per quanti
anni, nel tempo, furono gli amanti
60 presi e delusi dall'eterno inganno?

And poison's arts in others execute
a crimson miracle: hair becomes a flame
of electrical reflections without a name
swelling about the temples as they shoot . . .

Beautiful useless promises of a sweet
enticer of all our hunger, when a small
woman who doesn't care for us at all
can truss us up with chains at hands and feet,
when every day the hamstrung amorist
senses the best of life is going fast,
just as the grains of sand go slipping past
the squeezing fingers of a hollow fist . . .

We've met them everywhere: and at the play
in the evening, in the light that made us blind,
the lovely sweep of naked shoulders twined
our minds up with its magic potency:
and when the lights went down and shadows cast
encroaching darkness down along the rows,
the icy lightning of a necklace was
the index of a double treasure chest.

And they've been our companions, but for short
hours, on wordless journeys, on journeys back:
we've found them again days later, on our trek
through virgin snowfalls, in an Alpine hut.
We've found them again at the shore, beside the sea,
where the wounding hunger really ran us through:
for that sweet lady that we never knew
a night of sleepless hours along the sea! . . .

Who are those women, where are they going? Where
are all those nomads going? How many years
have all these lovers wasted all these tears,
caught up inside that everlasting snare?

Ah! Noi saremmo lieti d'un destino
impreveduto che ce le ponesse
a fianco, tristi e pellegrine anch'esse
nel nostro malinconico cammino.

65 Piú d'un inganno lasciò largo posto
a piú d'una ferita ancora viva...
Taluna – intatta – ci attirò furtiva
seco, ma per un utile nascosto;
altre, già quasi vinte, quasi dome,
70 nella nostra fiducia troppo inerte,
fantasticate quali prede certe,
furono salve, non sappiamo come...

Ed altre... Ma perché tanti ricordi
salgono dall'inutile passato?
75 Salgono col profumo del passato
da un cofanetto pieno di ricordi?
Ed ecco i segni, ecco le cose mute,
superstiti d'amori nuovi e vecchi,
lettere stinte, nastri, fiori secchi,
80 delle godute e delle non godute...

Desideri e stanchezze, indizi certi
d'un avvenire dedito all'ambascia
torbida che si schianta e che ci sfascia
rendendoci piú tristi e piú deserti...
85 Eppure, un giorno, questa febbre interna
parve svanire: quando ci si accorse,
tardi, di quella che sarebbe forse
per noi la sola vera amante eterna...

How glad we'd be if there would come to pass
some stroke of fate to set them at our side,
those women who walk our melancholy road
as sad and restless as the rest of us.

More than one temptress left us in the end
with more than one wound still throbbing vividly . . .
Someone—intact—allured us furtively
to her, but for an unpaid dividend.
Others, almost defenseless beneath our sway,
trusting in our assurances, helpless things
already possessed in our imaginings,
escaped, and we don't know how they got away . . .

And others . . . But why do all these memories
come rising up once more from a useless past,
come rising up with the perfume of the past
out of a casket filled with memories?
And look at the signs: mute objects in a void,
the relics of all those love affairs of ours,
the faded letters, ribbons, withered flowers
of the enjoyed and of the unenjoyed . . .

Desire and fatigue, the signs are bad:
trapped in a future of dreary hopelessness
till we come apart in one unholy mess,
left even more deserted and more sad . . .
And yet one day the fever seemed to be
finally breaking, when, at last, to us
appeared the woman who might be for us
the one true love through all eternity . . .

Tanto l'amammo per quel solo istante
90 ch'ella si volse pallida su noi
nell'offerta di un attimo, ma poi,
sparve, ella pure; sparve come tante
altre donne che passano, col viso
seminascosto dal cappello enorme
95 inasprendo la brama che non dorme
col baleno degli occhi e del sorriso...

For that one moment we were so possessed
with love for her, she turned to us within
the offer of an instant, but just then
she vanished, even she vanished, like all the rest
of the women who pass with faces all the while
half hidden by huge hats, those women who keep
rubbing the skin of a hunger that doesn't sleep
with the flashing of their eyes and a flashing smile . . .

«*Ex voto*»

S'alza la neve in pace;
la valle che s'imbianca
spicca sul cielo bruno.

Il Santuario tace
5 nella gran pace bianca
dove non c'è nessuno.

Nessuno per guarire
del male che lo strazia
piú giunge di lontano...

10 Sol io potrei salire,
salire per la grazia:
mi rifarebbe sano...

Ma non vedrò la faccia
nera e la mitra aguzza...
15 Troppo ai bei dí sereni,

avvinto a quelle braccia
baciai la medagliuzza
tepente tra i due seni...

Ex Voto

In stillness the snow lands,
the countryside turns pale
against a darkening sky.

The Sanctuary stands
in the wide peaceful vale
where no traveler comes by.

No traveler comes anymore
from far off to relieve
the sickness and the pain . . .

If only I could soar,
soar through grace: I believe
it would make me well again . . .

But I won't see the black face
and the many-pointed crown . . .
Clear days, too well I kissed

(enthralled in that embrace)
the medal that hung down
in the warmth between two breasts . . .

Ketty

I

Supini al rezzo ritmico del panka.

Sull'altana di cedro il giorno muore,
giunge dal Tempio un canto or mesto or gaio,
giungono aromi dalla jungla in fiore.

5 Bel fiore del carbone e dell'acciaio
Miss Ketty fuma e zufola giuliva
altoriversa nella sedia a sdraio.

Sputa. Nell'arco della sua saliva
m'irroro di freschezza: ha puri i denti,
10 pura la bocca, pura la genciva.

Cerulo-bionda, le mammelle assenti,
ma forte come un giovinetto forte,
vergine folle da gli error prudenti,

ma signora di sé della sua sorte
15 sola giunse a Ceylon da Baltimora
dove un cugino le sarà consorte.

Ma prima delle nozze, in tempo ancora
esplora il mondo ignoto che le avanza
e qualche amico esplora che l'esplora.

20 Error prudenti e senza rimembranza:
Ketty zufola e fuma. La virile
franchezza, l'inurbana tracotanza

attira il mio latin sangue gentile.

Ketty

I

We lie in the rhythmic breezes of the *panka*.

On the cedar terrace dies the afternoon:
from the Temple come now sad now joyous chants,
aromas come from the jungle now in bloom.

A beautiful bloom of mines and smelting plants,
Miss Ketty smokes and whistles next to me
sprawled in a deck chair in casual elegance.

She spits. In her saliva's trajectory
I'm lightly sprinkled with a dew that freshens:
her mouth, teeth, gums are pure as pure can be.

A blue-eyed blonde, her breasts too slight to mention,
but spunky as a boy at any rate,
a foolish virgin of prudent indiscretions

but mistress of herself and of her fate,
she's come to Ceylon alone from Baltimore
where with a cousin soon she'll celebrate

her wedding day. But in the time before
she explores the unknown world as it awaits,
and explores a friend, and lets the friend explore.

Prudent indiscretions and no regrets:
Ketty whistles and smokes. And I recline.
Her tough disdain, her impudent cigarettes

allure this genteel Latin blood of mine.

II

Non tocca il sole le pagode snelle
25 che la notte precipita. Le chiome
delle palme s'ingemmano di stelle.

Ora di sogno! E Ketty sogna: «... or come
vivete, se non ricco, al tempo nostro?
È quotato in Italia il vostro nome?
30 Da noi procaccia dollari l'inchiostro...»
«Oro ed alloro!...» – «Dite e traducete
il piú bel verso d'un poeta vostro...»

Dico e la bocca stridula ripete
in italo-brittanno il grido immenso:
35 «Due cose belle ha il mon... Perché ridete?»

«Non rido. Oimè! Non rido. A tutto penso
che ci dissero ieri i mendicanti
sul *grande amore* e sul *nessun compenso*.

(Voi non udiste, Voi tra i marmi santi
40 irridevate i budda millenari,
molestavate i chela e gli elefanti).

Vive in Italia, ignota ai vostri pari,
una casta felice d'infelici
come quei monni astratti e solitari.

45 Sui venti giri non degli edifici
vostri s'accampa quella fede viva,
non su gazzette, come i dentifrici;

II

The slim pagodas are shadowed one by one
as the sun draws darkness down. On every tree
the stars bejewel the palm leaves of Ceylon.

Hour of dreams. And Ketty dreams: ". . . I don't see
how you live, if you're not rich, in a time like this.
Has your name much currency back in Italy?

Writers are quite well paid in the U.S. . . ."
"Laurels and lucre!"—"Say for me and translate
one of your poets' loveliest lines of verse."

I say, and her high trill tries to imitate
in Anglo-Italian that deep human cry:
"*Due cose belle ha il mon* . . . Now wait!

You're laughing?"—"Oh no! I'm thinking of yesterday,
what those beggars told us, about 'no recompense,'
about 'great love,' and all they had to say . . ."

(You didn't hear. Among the marble saints
you mocked the ancient Buddhist statuary,
harassed the *chelas* and the elephants.)

". . . Unknown to you and yours, there lives a very
happy caste, in Italy, of hapless ones
ascetic like those monks and solitary.

Not in your skyscrapers with their swirling winds
do these few faithful plant their standards, nor
like ads for toothpaste in the public prints.

sete di lucro, gara fuggitiva,
elogio insulso, ghigno degli stolti
50 piú non attinge la beata riva;

l'arte è paga di sé, preclusa ai molti,
a quegli data che di lei si muore...»
Ma intender non mi può, benché m'ascolti,

la figlia della cifra e del clamore.

III

55 Intender non mi può. Tacitamente
il braccio ignudo premo come zona
ristoratrice, sulla fronte ardente.

Gelido è il braccio ch'ella m'abbandona
come cosa non sua. Come una cosa
60 non sua concede l'agile persona...

– «O yes! Ricerco, aduno senza posa
capelli illustri in ordinate carte:
l'Illustrious lòchs collection piú famosa.

Ciocche illustri in scienza in guerra in arte
65 corredate di firma o documento,
dalla Patti, a Marconi, a Buonaparte...

(mordicchio il braccio, con martirio lento
dal polso percorrendolo all'ascella
a tratti brevi, come uno stromento)

Competition run amuck, the itch for more,
smug fools, and praise so easy it's absurd—
they'll never bring you to that blessed shore.

Art is its own reward, not for the herd
but for those who live and die at the Muse's feet . . ."
But though she's listening, she can't hear a word,

daughter of ledgers and the scandal sheet.

III

She can't hear a word I tell her. Silent now
I take her arm and press it ardently,
like a medicinal band, to my burning brow.

How cool is the naked arm she lets fall free
like a thing not hers. And like a thing not hers
the nimble body that she yields to me . . .

—"Oh yes! I collect the locks of illustrious
people, and mount them all on little cards:
la famosissima hair *raccolta* that ever was.

Hairs from the heads of science and war and the arts
all backed by a signature or a document:
I've got Marconi's, Patti's, Bonaparte's . . ."

(I nibble her arm, with an agonized ascent
of slow small nibbles, as my mouth progresses
from pulse to armpit, like an instrument)

70 e voi potrete assai giovarmi nella
    Italia vostra, per commendatizie...»
    – «Dischiomerò per Voi l'Italia bella!»

    «Manca D'Annunzio tra le mie primizie;
    vane l'offerte furono e gl'inviti
75 per tre capelli della sua calvizie...»

    – «Vi prometto sin d'ora i peli ambiti;
    completeremo il codice ammirando:
    a maggior gloria degli Stati Uniti...».

    L'attiro a me (l'audacia superando
80 per cui va celebrato un cantarino
    napolitano, dagli Stati in bando...).

    Imperterrita indulge al resupino,
    al temerario – o Numi! – che l'esplora
    tesse gli elogi di quel suo cugino,

85 ma sui confini ben contesi ancora
    ben si difende con le mani tozze,
    al pugilato esperte... In Baltimora

    il cugino l'attende a giuste nozze.

". . . and you can really help me, with addresses
and introductions to people that you know . . ."
—"For you I'll leave all Italy shorn of tresses!"

"I haven't got a thing from D'Annunzio.
For all my pleas, that shiniest of pates
still wears the three hairs that I covet so . . ."

—"I promise you the hairs of all the greats
you long for: we'll complete this compilation
to the greater glory of the United States . . ."

I pull her upon me (outdoing that audacious
Neapolitan warbler who in recent days
has had to quit the States for a long vacation . . .).

Undaunted she admits the hand that strays
as I—O gods!—supine and bold, explore,
and in my ear she pours her cousin's praise,

but at that boundary many times before
contested, two blunt fists put up a fight,
defending her title . . . Back in Baltimore

the cousin expects a proper wedding night.

Notes to the Poems

The Colloquies
The epigraph is from lines 13-14 of "In the House of the Survivor." The lines allude to lines 99-100 of *Consalvo* by Giacomo Leopardi (1798-1837):

Due cose belle ha il mondo:
amore e morte.

The reference is the basis of a motif central to Gozzano's poetry in general and to the volume *The Colloquies* in particular.
 1.7: the biblical wonder: Joshua's making the sun stand still (Josh. 10:12-13).

The Two Roads
Reprinted with several omissions and revisions from *The Road to Shelter*.

Paul and Virginia
 The plot, the characters (although Gozzano omits another, wicked priest), the setting (Mauritius), and many of the details of the poem are drawn from the tremendously popular sentimental romance *Paul et Virginie* (1787) by Jacques-Henri Bernardin de Saint-Pierre (1737-1814).
 The epigraph, oddly enough, is the poem's last three lines.
 l.40: Jean-Jacques: Rousseau.
 l.73: your romantic tale: *Paul et Virginie*.

Signorina Felicita
 l.5: *Ivrea . . . Dora*: a village and a river in the Canavese, in Piedmont.
 l.32: the wanderer on the sea: Ulysses.
 l.41: Carolina Otero (1868-1953), popular ballerina.
 l.159: Torquato Tasso (1544-1595), epic poet.
 l.244: Seasons: statues representing the seasons.
 l.356: translated from line 4 of *La Ballade à la Lune* by Alfred de Musset (1810-1857).
 l.429: Giovanni Prati (1814-1884), perhaps best known for the sentimental love poetry of his early years.

Grandmother Speranza's Friend
 Reprinted with several omissions and revisions from *The Road to Shelter*.
 l.1: Vittorio Alfieri (1749-1803), poet and dramatist.
 l.9: Massimo d'Azeglio (1798-1866), Torinese painter, novelist, political fig-

ure. Manzoni's son-in-law, he was active in the Risorgimento. His unfinished memoirs, *I miei ricordi*, were published posthumously in 1867.

l.30: Arcangelo Corelli (1653-1713), Scarlatti (1660-1725).

l.32: Giordanello: Giuseppe Giordani (1744-1798).

l.46: Prati: see note to "Signorina Felicita," l. 429.

l.48: the Emperor: of Austria, ruler of the Italian kingdom of Lombardo-Venetia, 1815-1859. The uncle is a reactionary.

l.50: the King of Sardinia: Vittorio Emanuele II (1820-1878), who later (1861) became king of a unified Italy.

l.61: most likely Teresa Brambilla (1810-1859), soprano.

l.64: the premiere of *Rigoletto* took place on 11 March 1851.

l.67: Count Joseph Radetzky (1766-1858), Austrian field marshal who defeated the Sardinians in 1848 and 1849.

l.80: Clara Carrara Spinelli (1814-1886), Milanese hostess and wife of the poet Andrei Maffei (1798-1885).

l.88: *Tales Illustrated*: magazine of popular fiction.

l.89: Parisina (subject of a poem by Byron), wife of Niccolò III d'Este, beheaded in 1425 for incest with her stepson Ugo.

l.90: Werther: protagonist of the novel (1774) by Goethe. The woman he loves in vain is named Charlotte.

l.95: Giuseppe Mazzini (1805-1872), patriot and, for much of his life, exile.

l.102: Young Ortis: protagonist of *Ultime lettere di Jacopo Ortis* (1802), Werther-like novel by Ugo Foscolo (1778-1827).

Cocotte

"I've sketched out a poem, in hendecasyllabics and six-line stanzas; the poem is beautiful, the verses are ugly. It's a recollection of a *cocotte* I knew at Cornigliano Ligure, nearly twenty years ago (in 1889: I was five years old!). She was our next-door neighbor, since she was renting, for the baths, the other half of the villa that we were renting. But there was a railing between her garden and ours, and it was between the bars that she embraced me a few times, calling me '*Mon petit chéri!*' with a smile that I still remember, a smile in which she mourned all the longing of her unsatisfied motherhood. Then my family noticed us, they talked to me at the table, and I heard from my mother the word cocotte. . . . Since that time I've never seen my French friend, the wicked lady, again. I've seen Cornigliano again, however, just last week, and the garden of twenty years ago, and I felt a great need of her." Gozzano to Amalia Guglielminetti, 23 December 1907.

Totò Merúmeni

The name plays on the title of Terence's comedy *Heautontimorumenos* ("the self-tormentor"), and on Baudelaire's *L'Héautontimorouménos* in *Les Fleurs du Mal*.

ll.21-22: Petrarch, *Rime*, CCCLX, 80-81:

*Questi in sua prima età fu dato a l'arte
da vender parolette, anzi menzogne.*

Gozzano was lucky enough in *his* youth to find it unnecessary to "sell his little words, or better, his pack of lies."

ll.31-32: adaptation of a statement in *Also Sprach Zarathustra*.

A Woman Resurrected
l.64: the three reigns: of Nature (animal, vegetable, mineral).
l.95: "I'm musing many pages": the line looks forward to *Butterflies*, Gozzano's unfinished series of "entomological epistles."
ll.119-120: Dante, *Inferno*, XXX, 136-138:

*Qual è colui che suo dannaggio sogna,
  che, sognando, desidera sognare,
  sí che quel ch'è, come non fosse, agogna.*

("And as he is who dreams of his own harm,
  Who dreaming wishes it may be a dream,
  So that he craves what is, as if it were not." Longfellow)

Turin
l.12: good King Carlo Alberto: (1798-1849), King of Sardinia 1831-1849.
l.15: Eleonora Duse (1858-1924), perhaps the greatest actress of her time, best known for tragic roles written for her by her sometime lover, D'Annunzio.
l.19: the Barnabite order was founded in Milan in 1533.
ll.29-30: *Giacomo* is Leopardi. The citations are from his *L'infinito* and *Ricordanze* respectively. The implication is that there are worse places to be born, such as Leopardi's "savage native town" of Recanati.
ll.38-39: d'Azeglio, *I miei ricordi*: see note to "Grandmother Speranza's Friend," l.9.

August Rain
l.48: Dante, *Paradiso*, XXV, 7-8:

*con altra voce omai, con altro vello
ritornerò poeta.*

See also note to "A Woman Resurrected," l.95.

The Colloquies
l.10: an echo of the opening line of Dante's *Inferno*:

Nel mezzo del cammin di nostra vita

l.18: Virginia Oldoini Verasis, Contessa Castiglione (1835-1899).
l.35: Arthur and Friedrich: Schopenhauer and Nietzsche.

The Illiterate
Based on Bartolomeo Tarella, a caretaker at Meleto, the Gozzano family villa.
l.46: that great Book: not the Bible, but Nature.
l.164: *Lamarmora*: Generale Alfonso Ferrero di La Marmora (1804-1878) commanded the Sardinian expedition in the Crimean War.

Strength
Dedicated to Mario Bassi, who, in addition to his wrestling, was a Torinese poet, lecturer, literary journalist, and friend of a number of other poets.

The Last Renunciation
Gozzano adapted the situation and the structure of this poem from a text in a volume of Greek folk songs published in Italian translation in 1903.
The epigraph is from *La madre* by Giovanni Pascoli (1855-1912).

Parable of the Fruit (1904)
The epigraph—"Behold the handmaid of the Lord; be it unto me according to thy word"—is actually from the Gospel of St. Luke (1:38).

Demi-vierge (1905)
The title is a French expression whose meaning is approximated by the epithet in line 9. The dedicatee is unidentified.

The Pattern (c. 1906)
Deleted by Gozzano from the manuscript of *The Road to Shelter*.

Historia (c. 1907)
The title is Latin: "History; tale, story."

[Stecchetti] (c. 1907)
Gozzano never published this sonnet, whose title was supplied by later editors. "Lorenzo Stecchetti" is best known for *Postuma* (1877), a book of lyrics purportedly by a young poet recently dead of tuberculosis. The book, considered salacious by some, was actually the work of Olindo Guerrini (1845-1916), who, though nearly forty years his senior, outlived Gozzano by about ten weeks.

The Loveliest (c. 1909)
Several commentators have compared this poem to Ernest Dowson's "The Fortunate Islands," a prose poem in *Decorations* (1899). Despite obvious similarities of detail, Dowson's theme—"We have adventured, but we have not found anything . . . , and there is only one thing we expect. . . . We tell you the truth: there are no fortunate islands"—is counter to Gozzano's, though much more applicable to others of Gozzano's poems.
l.14: Tenerife and Palma are two of the Canary Islands.
l.16: Teide is a volcanic peak on Tenerife.

The Unenjoyed (c. 1909)
   The omission of this poem from *The Colloquies* is a bit strange, given its obvious tonal and thematic links with a number of the poems in that collection.

Ex voto (1910)
   The title is a Latin phrase expressive of a wish, desire, or vow. The sanctuary is that of Oropa, with its black statue of the Virgin. The elements of this poem—tuberculosis, Catholic yearnings, sensuality, a sense of personal damnation—combine to make it Gozzano's most *fin de siècle* production.

Ketty (c. 1913)
   l.1: *panka*: a large hanging fan.
   1.35: *Due cose belle ha il mon . . .* : see note to "The Colloquies," p. 245.
   l.41: *chela*: a pupil of a guru; a Buddhist novice.
   l.66: Adelina Patti (1843-1919), soprano.
   l.74: that shiniest of pates: as implied here, D'Annunzio was spectacularly bald.
   l.80: Neapolitan warbler: Enrico Caruso, who had been forced to leave the United States as a result of a judgment brought against him in a breach-of-promise suit.

Selected Bibliography

By Gozzano

Poetry

La via del rifugio. Torino: Streglio, 1907.
I colloqui. Milano: Treves, 1911.
Le poesie. Milano: Garzanti, 1960. Introductory essay by Eugenio Montale. Contains the two books and *Farfalle.*
Poesie. Torino: Einaudi, 1973. Ed. Edoardo Sanguinetti. The collected poetry: definitive text; excellent apparatus.
I colloqui e prose. Milano: A. Mondadori, 1974. Ed. Marziano Guglielminetti. The complete *I colloqui*, plus related materials, along with *Verso la cuna del mondo* and brief selections from crepuscular poets; fully annotated.
Poesie. Milano: Rizzoli, 1977. Ed. Giorgio Bárberi Squarotti. Based on Sanguinetti's edition.

Prose

I tre talismani. Ostiglia: La Scolastica editrice, 1914. Fairy tales.
Verso la cuna del mondo, lettere dall'India (1912-1913). Milano: Treves, 1917. Travel.
L'altare del passato. Milano: Treves, 1918. Short stories.
L'ultima traccia. Milano: Treves, 1919. Short stories.
Lettere d'amore di Guido Gozzano e Amalia Guglielminetti. Milano: Garzanti, 1951.
La moneta seminata e altri scritti. Milano: Scheiwiller, 1968. Uncollected fairy tales, plus variants of poems and reproductions of original printings and illustrations.
Lettere a Carlo Vallini con altri inediti. Torino: Centro di Studi Piemontesi, 1971.

Collected Editions

Opere. 5 vols. Milano: Treves, 1935-1937. Ed. P. Schinetti.
Opere. Milano: Garzanti, 1948. Ed. C. Calcaterra and A. de Marchi.

Poesie e prose. Milano: Garzanti, 1961. Ed. A. de Marchi. Revised and slightly expanded edition of the 1948 collection, but with the omission of many of its textual notes.

ABOUT GOZZANO

Biography and Reminiscence

Brusati, Massimo. *Incontri con Guido Gozzano.* Cortina d'Ampezzo: Circolo artistico di Cortina d'Ampezzo, 1951.
Gotta, Salvator. *Tre maestri: Fogazzaro, Giacosa, Gozzano.* Milano: A. Mondadori, 1975.
Martin, Henriette. *Guido Gozzano (1883-1916).* Paris: Presses Universitaires de France, 1968. Italian translation, Milano: Mursia, 1971. Basically analysis and criticism, but its first 120 pages present a biography.
Vaccari, Walter. *La vita e i pallidi amori di Guido Gozzano.* Milano: Omnia editrice, 1958. Sentimental and unreliable, but the only separate full-length life.

Criticism

The list of books and articles about Gozzano is a long one, and it stretches from 1907 to the present. What follows is a selection of books published in the last two decades.

Boni, Massimiliano. *Guido Gozzano e la poesia italiana del Novecento con altre note.* Bologna: Edizioni Italiane Moderne, 1971.
Lugnani, Lucio. *Gozzano.* Firenze: La Nuova Italia, 1973.
Marzot, Giulio. *D'Annunzio e Gozzano.* Bologna: Edizioni Italiane Moderne, 1979.
Mondo, Lorenzo. *Natura e storia in Guido Gozzano.* Milano: Silva, 1969.
Piromalli, Antonio. *Ideologia e arte in Guido Gozzano.* Firenze: La Nuova Italia, 1972.
Sanguinetti, Edoardo. *Guido Gozzano. Indagini e letture.* Torino: Einaudi, 1966.
———. *Tra liberty e crepuscolarismo.* Milano: Mursia, 1961.
Savoca, Giuseppe, and Mario Tropea. *Pascoli, Gozzano e i crepuscolari.* Bari: Editori Laterza, 1978.
Stäuble, Antonio. *Sincerità e artificio in Gozzano.* Ravenna: Longo, 1972.
Tedesco, Natale. *La condizione crepuscolare.* Firenze: La Nuova Italia, 1970.

In English

There are brief sketches and commentaries in histories of Italian literature and in the relevant biographical dictionaries of authors. In addition to these, there are three essays that constitute more than a page or two:

Nims, John Frederick. Essay on *Totò Merúmeni*. In *The Poem Itself*, ed. Stanley Burnshaw. New York: Holt, Rinehart and Winston, 1960. Nims presents a plain prose translation of and a running commentary on the poem, all set within an essay that provides some well-expressed insights and a useful synthesis of some artistic currents of Gozzano's time.

Phelps, Ruth Shepard. *Italian Silhouettes*. New York: Alfred A. Knopf, 1924. The chapter "Guido Gozzano's Book of Youth" is an impressionistic and somewhat florid discussion, mainly of *I colloqui*. Phelps also translates, among shorter bits and pieces, 32 lines of *Alle soglie* and 32 lines of the concluding *I colloqui*. The book also contains a chapter on Amalia Guglielminetti.

"A Return to Guido Gozzano: An Italian Poet Rediscovered." *Italy: Documents and Notes* 17 (1968):55-60. This article, in an English-language Italian publication, is poorly written (translated?) and almost entirely biographical in its emphasis. Despite the subtitle, Gozzano's poetry is hardly mentioned.

Other translations are:

Golino, Carlo, ed. *Contemporary Italian Poetry: An Anthology*. Berkeley and Los Angeles: University of California Press, 1962. Versions (by the editor) of *La differenza*, *I colloqui* (the opening poem), and *L'assenza*.

Paragallo, Elizabeth M. Versions of *I colloqui* (the opening poem) and *Elogio degli amori ancillari* in *Experiment* 4, no. 3 (Summer 1949): 274-275. A version of *Convito* in *Experiment* 5, no. 1 (Spring 1950): 340-341. The first two are reprinted in L. R. Lind, ed., *Twentieth-Century Italian Poetry* (Indianapolis and New York: Bobbs-Merrill, 1974), which also prints her versions of *Invernale* and *La signorina Felicita*.

Tusiani, Joseph, ed. and trans. *From Marino to Marinetti: An Anthology of Forty Italian Poets Translated into English Verse*. New York: Baroque Press, 1974. Versions of *La signorina Felicita*, *Totò Merúmeni*, and *Cocotte*.

THE LOCKERT LIBRARY OF POETRY
IN TRANSLATION

George Seferis: Collected Poems (1924-1955), translated, edited, and introduced by Edmund Keeley and Philip Sherrard

Collected Poems of Lucio Piccolo, translated and edited by Brian Swann and Ruth Feldman

C. P. Cavafy: Collected Poems, translated by Edmund Keeley and Philip Sherrard and edited by George Savidis

Benny Andersen: Selected Poems, translated by Alexander Taylor

Selected Poetry of Andrea Zanzotto, translated and edited by Ruth Feldman and Brian Swann

Poems of René Char, translated by Mary Ann Caws and Jonathan Griffin

Selected Poems of Tudor Arghezi, translated and edited by Michael Impey and Brian Swann

Tadeus Różewicz: The Survivor, translated and introduced by Magnus J. Krynski and Robert A. Maguire

"Harsh World" and Other Poems by Ángel González, translated by Donald D. Walsh

Dante's "Rime," translated and introduced by Patrick S. Diehl

Ritsos in Parentheses, translations and introduction by Edmund Keeley

Salamander: Selected Poems of Robert Marteau, translated and introduced by Anne Winters

Angelos Sikelianos. Selected Poems, translated and introduced by Edmund Keeley and Philip Sherrard

The Dawn is Always New: Selected Poetry of Rocco Scotellaro, translated by Ruth Feldman and Brian Swann

Selected Later Poems of Marie Luise Kaschnitz, translated by Lisel Mueller

Osip Mandelstam's "Stone," translated and introduced by Robert Tracy

The Man I Pretend to Be: "The Colloquies" and Selected Poems of Guido Gozzano, translated and edited by Michael Palma, with an introductory essay by Eugenio Montale

Library of Congress Cataloging in Publication Data
Gozzano, Guido, 1883-1916.
　The man I pretend to be.

　(Lockert library of poetry in translation)
　Bibliography: p.
　　I.　Palma, Michael, 1945-　　　II.　Title.
PQ4817.09A26　　　851'.912　　　80-8551
ISBN 0-691-06467-9
ISBN 0-691-01378-0 (pbk.)